Why the World Does Not Exist

Why the World Does Not Exist

Markus Gabriel

Translated by Gregory S. Moss

polity

First published in German as *Warum es die Welt nicht gibt* © Ullstein Buchverlage GmbH, Berlin, 2013

Polity Press
65 Bridge Street
Cambridge CB2 1UR, UK

Polity Press
350 Main Street
Malden, MA 02148, USA

ISBN-13: 978-0-7456-8756-8

A catalogue record for this book is available from the British Library.
Library of Congress Cataloging-in-Publication Data

Gabriel, Markus, 1980-
  [Warum es die welt nicht gibt. English]
  Why the world does not exist / Markus Gabriel. -- English edition.
    pages cm
  Translation of: Warum es die welt nicht gibt.
  Includes bibliographical references and index.
  ISBN 978-0-7456-8756-8 (hardback : alk. paper) 1. Ontology. 2. Postmodernism. 3. Philosophy, Modern--21st century. I. Title.

  BD311.G3313 2015
  111--dc23

Typeset in 11/13 Sabon by
Servis Filmsetting Ltd, Stockport, Cheshire
Printed and bound in the UK by CPI Group (UK) Ltd, Croydon

The publisher has used its best endeavours to ensure that the URLs for external websites referred to in this book are correct and active at the time of going to press. However, the publisher has no responsibility for the websites and can make no guarantee that a site will remain live or that the content is or will remain appropriate.

Every effort has been made to trace all copyright holders, but if any have been inadvertently overlooked the publisher will be pleased to include any necessary credits in any subsequent reprint or edition.

For further information on Polity, visit our website: politybooks.com

Contents

Thinking Philosophy Anew

Life, the universe, and everything else . . . presumably everyone has asked themselves what it all means. Where do we find ourselves? Are we only an aggregation of elementary particles in a gigantic world receptacle? Or do our thoughts, wishes, and hopes have a distinct reality – and, if so, what? How can we understand our existence or even existence in general? And how far does our knowledge extend?

In this book I will develop the outlines of a new philosophy, which follows from a simple, basic thought, namely the idea that the world does not exist. As you will see, this does not mean that nothing exists at all. There are planets, my dreams, evolution, the toilet flush, hair loss, hopes, elementary particles, and even unicorns on the far side of the moon, to mention only a few examples. The principle that the world does not exist entails that everything else exists. For this reason, I can already announce that I will claim, as my first principle, that everything exists except one thing: the world.

The second principle of this book is NEW REALISM. New realism describes a philosophical stance that designates the era after so-called postmodernity (which I heralded in the summer of 2011 – strictly speaking, on 23 June 2011 around 1:30 p.m. – during a lunch in Naples with the Italian philosopher Maurizio Ferraris).[1]

1

In the first instance, then, new realism is nothing more than the name for the age after postmodernity.

Postmodernity was the radical attempt to start afresh after all of humanity's great promises had failed: from religion to modern science and all the way to the excessively radical ideas of left- and right-wing totalitarianism. Postmodernity wanted to consummate the break with tradition altogether and free us from the illusion that life has a specific meaning* after which we should all strive. In order to free us from this illusion, however, it merely fabricated new illusions – in particular the illusion that we are to a certain extent transfixed by our illusions. Postmodernity wanted to make us believe that, since prehistory, humanity has suffered from a gigantic collective hallucination – metaphysics.

Appearance and Being

One can define METAPHYSICS as the attempt to develop a theory of the world as such. Its aim is to describe how the world really is, not how the world seems to be or how it appears to us. In this way, metaphysics, to a certain extent, invented the world in the first place. When we speak about "the world," we mean everything that actually is the case, or, put differently: actuality. At this point, it is tempting to eliminate human beings from the equation "the world = everything that is actually the case." For one assumes that there is a differ-

---

* The original German is "einen Sinn des Lebens." Literally, one could take this as "the sense of life." Gabriel employs the same term, "Sinn," in his discussion of fields of sense and the senses. However, in this context, he is referring to what in English is usually spoken of as "the meaning of life" in philosophical contexts. For this reason, "Sinn" is taken as "meaning" in contexts where this is the more natural translation, such as in the "meaning of art" or the "meaning of religion." Throughout the book Gabriel plays on various senses of "sense" or "Sinn."

ence between things as they appear to us and how they actually are. Thus, in order to find out how they really are, one must, so to speak, remove everything that is added by man in the process of knowing.

Metaphysics has been criticized and rejected by many thinkers over the last centuries. The most recent and radical attempt to get rid of it in one stroke was post-modernism – that is, essentially, the idea that we live in an entirely post-metaphysical age, an age defined by the alleged fact that we have given up believing in the idea of a reality hidden behind the appearances. One could say that postmodernism's objection against metaphysics was that things exist only insofar as they appear to us. Accordingly, there is absolutely nothing further behind the appearances, no world or actuality in itself. Some less radical postmodernists, such as the American philosopher Richard Rorty, thought that there might in fact still be something behind the world as it appears to us. However, he thought that this could play no role for us as human beings, so he instead suggested that we increase solidarity among human beings rather than look for ultimate Truth (with a capital T) or ultimate Reality (with a capital R).

However, postmodernism, arguably, was only yet another variation on the basic themes of metaphysics – in particular, because postmodernism was based on a very general form of constructivism. CONSTRUCTIVISM assumes that there are absolutely no facts in themselves and that we construct all facts through our multifaceted forms of discourse and scientific methods. There is no reality beyond our language games or discourses; they somehow do not really talk about anything, but only about themselves. The most important source and fore-father of this tradition is Immanuel Kant. Kant indeed claimed that we could not know the world as it is in itself. No matter what we know, he thought that it would always in some respect have been made by human beings.

Let us take an example that is often used in this context, namely colors. Ever since Galileo Galilei and Isaac Newton, it has been suspected that colors do not actually exist. This assumption so exasperated colorful characters such as Goethe that he composed his own *Doctrine of Colors*. One might think that colors are only waves of a determinate length that strike our sensory receptors. The world in itself is actually completely without color, and it consists only of elementary particles which appear to us on a medium-sized scale where they somehow mutually stabilize one another into structures we perceive as bodies extended in space and time. It is exactly this thesis that is a widespread form of metaphysics in our time. It claims that, in itself, the world is completely different than it appears to us. Now Kant was still much more radical. He claimed that even this assumption (or perhaps supposition?) – about particles in space-time – is only a way in which the world, as it is in itself, appears to us. How it actually is, that is something we could absolutely never discover. Everything that we know is made by us, and just because of this we are also able to know it. In a famous letter to his fiancée, Wilhelmine von Zenge, Heinrich von Kleist illustrates Kantian Constructivism in the following way:

> If, instead of eyes, all men had green glasses they would have to conclude that the objects which they perceived through them were green; and they would never be able to decide whether their eyes were showing them the objects as they really existed or whether they were not adding something to those objects which did not belong to them but to their eyes. The same thing applies to the understanding. We cannot decide whether what we call truth really is truth or whether it only appears to us as such.[2]

Constructivism believes in Kant's "green glasses." To this, postmodernism added that we wear not only one but, rather, many glasses: science, politics, language games of love, poetry, various natural languages, social conventions, and so on. Everything is only a complicated play of illusions in which we mutually assign each other a place in the world, or, simply expressed: postmodernity deemed human existence to be a long French art-house film, in which all participants strive to seduce one another, to gain power over others, and to manipulate them. With clever irony this cliché is being called into question in contemporary French film. One thinks, for example, about Jean-Claude Brisseau's *Secret Games* or Catherine Breillat's *Anatomy of Hell*. This option is rejected, in a playful and amusing way, in David O. Russell's film *I ♥ Huckabees*, a film which, next to classics such as *Magnolia*, bears one of the best witnesses for new realism.

But human existence and knowledge is not a collective hallucination, nor are we transfixed in any picture worlds or conceptual systems behind which the real world is located. New realism assumes that we recognize the world as it is in itself. Of course we can be mistaken, for in some situations we indeed find ourselves in an illusion. But it is simply not the case that we are always or almost always mistaken.

New Realism

In order to understand to what extent new realism engenders a new orientation to the world, let us choose a simple example: let us assume that Astrid is currently standing in Sorrento and sees Vesuvius, while we (that is you, dear reader, and I) are currently in Naples and are also viewing Vesuvius. In this scenario there is Vesuvius, Vesuvius seen by Astrid (that is, from Sorrento), and Vesuvius seen by us (that is, from Naples). Metaphysics claims that, in this scenario, there is only one real object, namely Vesuvius. It just so happens that Vesuvius is being viewed in one instance from Sorrento and in another instance from Naples, which hopefully leaves it cold. Whoever might be interested in this is of no concern to Vesuvius. That is metaphysics.

In contrast, constructivism assumes that there are three objects in this scenario: Astrid's Vesuvius, your Vesuvius, and my Vesuvius. Beyond that there is absolutely no object or thing in itself – at least, no object which we could ever hope to know – as all objects which we can know anything about are supposed to be constructed by us.

In contrast, new realism supposes that, in this scenario, there are at least four objects:

1 Vesuvius
2 Vesuvius viewed from Sorrento (Astrid's perspective)
3 Vesuvius viewed from Naples (your perspective)
4 Vesuvius viewed from Naples (my perspective).

One can easily clarify why this option is the best. It is not only a fact that Vesuvius is a volcano that is located at a particular place on the earth's surface, which presently belongs to Italy, but it is also just as much with the same right a fact that it looks a certain way from Sorrento and another way from Naples. Even my most secret feelings while looking at the volcano are facts (even though they remain a secret only until a futuristic App for the iPhone 1000 + manages to scan my thoughts and put them online). New realism assumes that thoughts about facts exist with the same right as the facts at which our thoughts are directed. Thoughts about facts are just more facts. There is no reason to disdain thought, mind, consciousness, or human existence in general on the basis of the notion that the world would be exactly the way it is regardless of our presence in it. The moon is not more real than my beliefs about it; it does not have more right to be treated as existing. It will exist for longer than I will, but that does not matter for the question whether or not something exists.

In contrast, both metaphysics and constructivism fail because of an unjustified simplification of reality, in which they understand reality unilaterally either as *the world without spectators* or, equally one-sided, as *the world of spectators*. The world which I know is but always a world with spectators, in which facts that have no interest in me exist together with my interests (and perceptions, feelings, and so on). The world is neither exclusively the world without spectators nor the world of spectators. This is new realism. Old realism – that is, metaphysics – was only interested in the world without spectators, while constructivism quite narcissistically grounded the world and everything that is the case on our fantasies. Both theories lead to nothing.

Thus, one must explain how there can be spectators in a world in which spectators do not exist at all times and in all places – a problem that is solved in this book through the introduction of a new ontology. By ONTOLOGY one traditionally understands the "doctrine of being." In English, the ancient Greek participle "*to on*" means "being," and "*logos*" in this context simply means "doctrine." Ontology ultimately concerns the meaning of existence. What are we actually claiming when we say, for example, that there are meerkats? Many people believe that this question is addressed to physicists or, more generally, to natural scientists. In the end, everything that exists could just be material. After all, we don't seriously believe in ghosts, which can arbitrarily violate natural laws and unrecognizably whirl around us. (Well, most of us don't believe this.) However, if for this reason we claim that only that which can be investigated by natural science exists and can be dissected, or pictured, by means of the scalpel, microscope, or brain scanner, we would have missed the mark by a long shot. For in this case the federal state of Germany would not exist, nor would the future, numbers, or my dreams. But, because they do, we justifiably hesitate to entrust the question of Being to physicists. As it will be shown, physics is, well, biased.

The Plurality of Worlds

Presumably, since the beginning of this book you have wanted to know exactly what it means to claim that the world does not exist. I don't want to keep you in suspense any longer, and for this reason I anticipate what will later be proven with the help of reproducible thought experiments, examples, and paradoxes. One might think that the world is the domain of all those things that simply exist without our assistance and that surround us in this way. Nowadays, for example, we speak meaningfully of "the universe," by which we mean that most likely infinite expanse in which countless suns and planets run their orbit and in which people, in a quiet arm of the Milky Way, have built up their civilization. In point of fact, the universe too exists. I will not claim that there are no galaxies or black holes. But I do claim that the universe is not the whole. Strictly speaking, the universe is somewhat provincial.

By the UNIVERSE, I understand the experimentally accessible OBJECT DOMAIN of the natural sciences. Yet the world is considerably bigger than the universe. If the world is really absolutely everything, then governments, dreams, unrealized possibilities, works of art, and notably our thoughts about the world also belong to it. Thus, a good number of objects exist which man cannot touch. Just now, as you comprehend the thoughts which I have introduced to you, you do not suddenly disappear and peer, so to speak, from the outside onto the world whole. Our thoughts about the world remain in the world, for unfortunately it is not so easy to escape from this mess through reflection alone!

But even if governments, dreams, unrealized possibilities, and most notably our thoughts about the world also belong to the world, they cannot be identical to the object domain of the natural sciences. In any case, I am not aware that physics or biology have recently integrated sociology, law, or German language and cultural studies. Nor have I heard that the *Mona Lisa* has been taken apart in a chemistry lab. In any case, this would be quite expensive and also quite absurd. Hence, a first step in the right direction is to designate the world as all-encompassing, as the domain of all the domains mentioned above. Consequently, the world would be the domain in which there exist not only all things and facts which occur without us, but also all the things and facts which occur only with us. For ultimately it should be the domain that comprises everything – life, the universe, and everything else.

Still, to be precise, this all-inclusive being, the world, does not exist and cannot exist. With this main thesis, not only should the illusion that there is a world, to which humanity quite obstinately adheres, be destroyed, but at the same time I wish to use this in order to win positive knowledge from it. For I claim not only that the world does not exist but also that everything exists except the world.

That might sound a bit strange, but it can be easily illustrated, perhaps surprisingly, with the help of our everyday experiences. Let us imagine that we meet friends for dinner at a restaurant. Is there a domain here that encompasses all other domains? Can we, so to speak, draw a circle around everything that belongs to our visit to the restaurant? Now, take a look: we are presumably not the only ones in the restaurant. There are, as it turns out, several customers at the tables, with different group dynamics, preferences, and so on. In addition, there is the world of the employees, the restaurant owner, the cooks, as well as the world of the insects and spiders and the invisible bacteria that live in the restaurant. What is more, there are events at the subatomic level such as cell divisions, indigestion, and hormonal fluctuations. Some of these events and objects hang together, others not at all. What does the spider in the roof beams, unnoticed by all, know about my good mood or my eating preferences? And still the spider is a component of my visit to the restaurant, even if it mostly goes unnoticed. The same applies to digestion problems unless they are the center of attention.

There are also at the restaurant many domains of objects, small isolated worlds, as it were, that exist next to each other without really finding common ground. Thus, there are many small worlds, but not the one world to which they all belong. This does not mean that the many small worlds are only perspectives on one world, but that only the many small worlds exist. They actually exist, not merely in my imagination.

One can understand the claim that the world does not exist precisely in this sense. It is simply false that everything is connected. The popular claim that the fluttering of a butterfly's wings in Brazil, under certain circumstances, may cause a tornado in Texas is just untrue. Many things are connected with many other things, but it is false (in the strict sense, actually impossible!) that everything is connected. Of course every single one of us makes enduring connections. We produce images of ourselves and our surroundings, and we situate our interests in our environment. When, for example, we are hungry, we create a dinner menu out of our environment – the world becomes a feeding trough. At other moments we attentively follow a train of thought (I hope that this is just such a moment). Again, at other times we have completely different goals. In the process we tell ourselves that we always move in the same world, for which it is a prerequisite that we take ourselves to be sufficiently important. Our everyday business dealings seem to us, in the same way as it is for toddlers, infinitely important, and in a certain way they are. For we have only one life, which is taking place in a very short time span. Still, we can remember how things which today we take to be trifles – dandelions, for example – were infinitely important when we were children. In our own life, too, the connections are constantly dislocated. We change our self-image and the image of our surroundings and adapt at each moment to a situation that has not previously been there.

By analogy, so it is with the world as a whole. This exists just as little as a connection which encompasses all connections. There is simply no rule or world formula that describes everything. This is not contingent on the fact that we have not yet found it, but on the fact that it cannot exist at all.

Less than Nothing

Here we return to the difference between metaphysics, constructivism and new realism. The metaphysicians claim there is an all-encompassing rule, and the more courageous among them also claim they have finally found it. Accordingly, in the history of Occidental thought, one explorer of an alleged world formula has followed the next for almost three thousand years: from Thales of Miletus to Karl Marx and Stephen Hawking.

Constructivism, to the contrary, claims that we cannot know the rule. In its eyes, while we attempt to reach an agreement about which illusion we want to be applied, we find ourselves entangled in power struggles or communicative actions.

New realism, in contrast, attempts consistently and seriously to answer the question whether, in principle, such a rule could exist. The answer to this question is thereby not merely a further construction. Instead it demands – as does every answer to every ordinary, serious, and well-meant question – to ascertain what the situation is. It would be odd if someone, in response to the question "Is there still some butter in the fridge?," answered you by saying: "Yes, but the butter and the fridge are actually only an illusion, a human construction. In truth neither the butter nor the fridge exists. At the very least, we don't know whether they exist. Nevertheless, enjoy your meal!"

In order to understand why the world does not exist, one must first understand what it means for something to exist at all. The apparently obvious answer is that something exists only when it is found in the world. Where should anything exist, if not in the world, when by this we understand the whole, the domain, in which everything takes place, whatever happens. That said, the world itself is not found in the world. At least I have never yet seen, tasted, or felt the world. And even when we think about the world, the world *about which* we think is obviously not identical with the world *in which* we think. For, while I think about the world right now, for example, this is merely a small event in the world, my little world-thought. Next to this there are still innumerable other objects and events: rain showers, toothaches, and the Federal Republic of Germany.

Thus, if we think about the world, what we grasp is something different than what we want to grasp. We can never grasp the whole. It is in principle too big for any thought. But this is not some defect of our capacity to know, neither is it immediately connected to the fact that the world is infinite (we can partially encompass the infinite, for example, in the form of calculus or set theory). Rather, the world cannot in principle exist because it is not found in the world.

On the one hand, therefore, I claim that less exists

than one would have expected, for the world does not exist. It does not exist and cannot exist. From this I will draw important consequences which, among other things, speak against the scientific worldview* in its contemporary, medial, and widespread socio-political version. I will argue against that worldview on the basis that one cannot produce a picture of the world, because it does not exist. All worldviews are equally misguided insofar as they ground our beliefs in a commitment to an overall world that already settles all big questions behind our backs. It does not matter whether one defers to God or to science when it comes to one's worldview. The problem is that one holds a worldview at all.

On the other hand, I also claim that considerably more exists than one would have expected – namely, everything else except the world. I claim that there are unicorns on the far side of the moon that are wearing police uniforms. For this thought exists in the world and with it the unicorns that are wearing police uniforms. To my knowledge, in contrast, they are not found in the universe. One does not find the aforementioned unicorns by booking a trip to the moon with NASA in order to photograph them. Nevertheless, how does it stand regarding all of the other things that allegedly do not exist: elves, witches, weapons of mass destruction in Luxembourg, and so on? Yes, these are also found in the world, for example in fairy tales, but not in Hamburg. Weapons of mass destruction do exist in the USA, but – as far as I know – not in Luxembourg. The question is never simply whether something exists but always

---

* The term that translated as "worldview" is "Weltbild," not "Weltanschauung," though more literally it is "world picture." The German echoes Heidegger's use of the term in *Die Zeit des Weltbildes*. Because it is the more common way of discussing what Gabriel is addressing, in addition to the fact that he is addressing those who explicitly appeal to "views" of the world, "worldview" is preferred over "world picture." Besides this, "worldview" reads more naturally.

where something exists. For everything that exists, exists somewhere – even if it is only in our imagination. Again, the one exception is the world. This we cannot imagine at all. What we imagine when we believe in the world is, as in the apt title of a recent book by the star philosopher Slavoj Žižek, so to speak, "less than nothing."[3]

In this book I would like to present the main features of a new, realistic ontology. Thus, it does not primarily concern other theories – I will introduce these only in places where some background may be helpful for greater understanding. It is thus not a general introduction to philosophy or a history of epistemology but an attempt to develop the outlines of a new philosophy in a way that is intelligible to readers who are interested in the questions dealt with, regardless of whether they might have a philosophical training. One need not first struggle through virtually unintelligible classics of philosophy in order to understand what is going on here. My aim is to write this book in such a way that it is readable without presuppositions.

It begins, like every philosophy, at the beginning. For this reason, the most important concepts, among other things, I employ will be as clearly defined as possible. The most important concepts are set in capital letters, and their meaning can be looked up in the glossary. I promise you that presumptuous philosophical monstrosities such as "the transcendental synthesis of apperception" will only show up in those sentences in which I promise you that they do not show up in this book.

Ludwig Wittgenstein once said that "What can be said at all can be said clearly."[4] I subscribe to this ideal, for philosophy should be not an elite esoteric science but, to a large extent, a public business even when it is sometimes quite long-winded. For this reason I confine myself to the following: to offer you a truly original path

(as I see it) through the labyrinth of perhaps the greatest philosophical questions: Where do we come from?
Where do we find ourselves? And what does it all mean?

The hope of being able to say something really new
about these questions of humanity may appear a bit
naïve, but, then again, the questions *are* themselves
naïve. Not infrequently it is children who pose these –
and hopefully will never stop asking them. The first two
philosophical questions I asked myself both occurred to
me on the way home from elementary school, and they
have never let go of me. Once when a raindrop fell in
my eye I saw through it a lantern doubled. Thus, I asked
myself the question whether I was actually seeing one
lantern or two, and how and to what extent I could trust
my senses. The second question occurred to me when all
of a sudden I realized that time passes, and that I could
identify completely different situations with the word
"now." At that moment I came upon the idea that the
world does not exist. I have needed a good twenty years
to penetrate this idea philosophically and to differentiate it from the idea that everything is only an illusion, or
that life is nothing but a dream.

In the meanwhile, for a few years I have been teach-
ing the discipline of philosophy at various universities,
and on innumerable occasions I have argued about the
problems of epistemology and philosophical skepticism
(my area of specialty) with researchers from around
the world. It may hardly surprise you that I have pretty
much doubted everything that I have encountered (perhaps most frequently my own convictions). But in the
process one thing has become clearer to me: the task of
philosophy is to start over from the beginning time and
time again.

I

What is this Actually: the World?

So, let us start over again! What does it all mean? This is the fundamental philosophical question per se. One day we came into a world without knowing where we came from or where we were going. Then, through upbringing and habituation, we found our way in our world. And as soon as we had become accustomed to this situation we mostly forgot to ask what it all means. What is this actually, the world?

In our life, our interactions, hopes, and wishes, as a rule, make sense. For example, as I write these words I am sitting in the carriage of a train in Denmark. Someone next to me is writing a text message, the train attendant is walking back and forth, and now and again I hear an announcement in Danish. All of this makes sense, since I am traveling to Aarhus, a city in northern Denmark, for which I am using a train, and on the trip I am experiencing what usually pertains to a train ride. Now let us imagine an alien being that is 88 feet tall and consists of a green liquid substance who comes to earth and gets on board the same train. To this being, everything would appear quite remarkable, maybe even completely unintelligible. It crawls through the narrow passages of my carriage and is astonished by all the new impressions (and especially by the hairy animals which sit in the compartments and tap a small screen frantically with their fingers).

Philosophers view the world to a certain extent in the same way as do alien beings or children. Everything is always completely new. They mistrust strongly ingrained judgments, and, yes, they even mistrust the scientific claims of experts. For starters, philosophers believe just about nothing at all. Accordingly, let us follow the model of a great philosophical hero: Socrates. In his famous defense before the Athenian court Socrates asserts: "I know that I know nothing."[5] In this respect, at least, nothing has changed for philosophers.

All the same, one can still learn a lot from philosophy; in particular one can learn never to forget that things could be very different from how they appear to us. Philosophy incessantly calls everything into question, even philosophy itself. And only in this way is it possible to understand what it all actually means. If one occupies oneself intensely with philosophy and its big questions, then one learns to scrutinize what is allegedly self-evident – an approach which, by the way, stands behind all the great accomplishments of humanity. If no one had ever posed the question "How should we live together?," then democracy and the idea of the free community would never have developed. If no one had ever posed the question "Where are we actually?," then we would still not yet know that the earth is round and the moon is only a revolving rock. On account of this claim, the philosopher Anaxagoras was charged with blasphemy. And Giordano Bruno, the great Italian philosopher, was condemned as a heretic because he was of the opinion that extra-terrestrial life exists and that the universe is infinite. This appeared irreconcilable with Christian theology, which assumed that the human being and the earth were the focus of God's interest, and God created the world at a particular moment in time (on account of which it was not allowed to be infinite).

Thus, the leading question of this book is What does it all mean? Does human life, human history, and human knowledge have any meaning at all? Are we only animals on some planet – cosmic ants or pigs in outer space? Are we simply very strange beings, who are just as alarming to strange aliens as the aliens (in the film with the same name) are to us?

If we want to find out what it all means we must first of all not forget what we believe we know, and begin afresh. The great French philosopher and scientist René Descartes rightly characterized the basic philosophical approach that at least once in one's life one ought to call into question everything that one has believed. At least once, we should put aside our usual convictions and ask – like aliens or children – where we actually find ourselves. For, before we ask ourselves the question "What does it all *mean*?," it seems sensible to answer the question concerning what the whole actually *is*.

In *Buddha's Little Finger* (2009), a popular contemporary Russian novel, a character with the significant name "Pjotr Pustota" (in English, "Peter Emptiness") makes the following observation: Moscow is located in Russia; Russia is located on two continents; the continents are located on the earth; the earth is located in the Milky Way; and the Milky Way is located in the universe. But where is the universe located? Where is the domain in which all of the entities mentioned above are located? Is it located, perhaps, only in our thoughts which contemplate this domain? But where are our thoughts located? If the universe is located in our thoughts, these cannot be located in the universe. Or is this not the case? Let us take heed of the two protagonists in their Socratic conversation:

> We clinked glasses and drank.
>   "And where is the Earth?"
>   "In the Universe."
>   "And where is the Universe?"
>   I thought for a second. "In itself."

"And where is this in itself?"

"In my consciousness."

"Well then, Petka, that means your consciousness is in your consciousness, doesn't it?"

"It seems so."

"Right," said Chapaev, straightening his moustache. "Now listen to me carefully. Tell me, what place is it in?"

"I do not understand, Vasily Ivanovich . . . The concept of place is one of the categories of consciousness, and so . . ."

"Where is this place? In what place is this concept of place located?"

"Well now, let us say that it is not really a place. We could call it a real . . ."

I stopped dead. Yes, I thought, that is where he is leading me. If I use the word "reality", he will reduce everything to my own thoughts once again. And then he will ask where they are located. I will tell him they are in my head, and then . . . A good gambit.[6]

With that Peter grasped the dizzying thought that the world does not exist. In the end, everything takes place in a great nowhere. In this novel, the title of which is *Chapayev and the Void*, its famous author, the Russian novelist Viktor Olegovich Pelevin, gives us an answer to our question "Where are we?": we are located in the universe, and this is located in emptiness, in nowhere. Everything is surrounded by a great emptiness, which reminds us of *The Neverending Story* by Michael Ende, in which the childish world of fantasy, Fantastica, is constantly threatened with destruction by the Nothing. Everything takes place only in our imagination, and outside of this exists the Nothing that constantly threatens it. For this reason, the message of the novel, as is well known, is that we must nourish and care for the world of childhood fantasy and as adults should not cease to dream, for otherwise we may fall victim to the Nothing, a completely meaningless reality, in which nothing has any meaning any more.

Philosophy is concerned with the questions that are raised through novels such as *Buddha's Little Finger* and *The Neverending Story*, through films such as Christopher Nolan's *Inception* or Rainer Werner Fassbinder's television film *World on a Wire*, which is the incomparably better precursor of *The Matrix*. These questions were not only raised in postmodern novels or in the popular culture of the twentieth and twenty-first centuries. The question as to whether reality is only a kind of gigantic illusion, a mere dream, has left deep tracks in the history of the human spirit. For thousands of years it has been posed wherever there has been religion, philosophy, poetry, painting and science.

In addition, modern science calls a great portion of reality into question, namely that reality which we experience with the help of our senses. In early modernity Galileo Galilei, for example, another Italian condemned to heresy, already doubted that colors existed independently of our sensations and claimed that reality was colorless and was constituted by mathematically describable material objects and changes in their spatial location. Modern theoretical physics is even more radical. So-called string theorists assume that reality is ultimately not spatio-temporal in any sense that is familiar to us. Regarding four-dimensional space-time, it could at the very least concern a type of hologram that is being projected from higher dimensions through determinate processes that are describable in terms of physical equations.[7]

That reality is other than it appears is a familiar idea to the modern person, one which was brought home to us in school, for example, when in amazement we realized for the first time that calculations can be formed with letters (variables) and not just with numbers. Or on trips, when we feel ourselves compelled to revise deep-seated prejudices. When, at a closer glance, so many objects are questionable, when all knowledge seems to be clothed in a kind of deep unknowing, why do we still place any trust at all in reality as it appears to us, in the world in which we seem to live?

You and the Universe

In this chapter I would like to investigate in more detail the question "Where does everything actually take place?," and answer it philosophically. In order to answer this question rationally, we must first differenti-ate two concepts concerning which confusion reigns in science, in everyday life, but also in philosophy – I mean the concepts "world" and "universe."

Let us begin with the universe. This concept is cur-rently loaded with mystical and religious connotations. For example, in esoteric bestsellers such as *The Cosmic Ordering Service* or contemporary films and television series (especially common, for example, in the popular sitcom *How I Met Your Mother*), the universe is seen as the place of destiny. The universe wants something from us or communicates something to us. Here the universe stands for the maximal whole in which we are located. If we ask ourselves what reality, actuality, the world, the cosmos or the universe are, we are asking somewhat vaguely about what the whole is and, subsequently, wondering what it means.

The question concerning the meaning of life and the question concerning the actual being of the whole are closely connected. If one assumes from the beginning that the whole is actually only a huge heap of subatomic particles or even crazier structures – such as a myriad of so-called strings that vibrate in multiple dimensions of time and space and appear according to the frequency of something like an electron or whatever – it will be correspondingly difficult to derive from that any meaning, because our life itself appears as a mere illusion, as a mere effect of spiritless particles. If I take for granted that I am only a heap of vibrating strings who imagines himself to be a human being with certain interests, plans, wishes, fears, etc., the Nothing from *The Neverending Story* has already overtaken me.

When we speak of the universe, we implicitly give an answer to the question concerning the being of the whole in which we find ourselves. Unlike so many mystics, we generally imagine the universe as a gigantic aggregation of galaxies and other various astronomical entities which light up against a dark background. Our picture of the universe looks like a gigantic photograph taken from something akin to the Hubble Telescope. And in this universe we are also found in one specific place – strictly speaking, on the third planet of a solar system that, together with at least 100 billion other stars, is part of the Milky Way.

At first glance this appears to be a relatively unproblematic description of our location. Something of the order: I am sitting in my living room on Helenenbergstrasse in Sinzig am Rhein, a small town in Germany. But that is misleading. There is a basic difference we must acknowledge whenever we are speaking about living rooms or planets. Planets and galaxies are objects of astronomy, and in that regard of physics, while living rooms are not. It pertains to the difference between living rooms and planets that we furnish living rooms, eat there, iron, or watch television, while we observe planets, measure their chemical composition through applied experiments, determine their distance from other astronomical entities, and much more. Physics concerns itself not with living rooms but, at best, with physical objects in living rooms, insofar as these fall under natural laws. Living rooms are simply not found in physics, though planets are.

Thus, living rooms and planets do not belong to the same domain of objects at all. A domain of objects is a domain which contains particular kinds of objects, in which rules obtain that link these objects with one another. There is, for example, the object domain of politics. Voters, community festivals, the so-called basis of the parties, tax dollars, and much more belong to this domain. There is also the domain of whole numbers, to which the numbers 7 and 5 belong and to which certain fundamental laws of arithmetic apply. In that respect, domains of objects are not necessarily spatially defined. The mayor of Oberwesel can travel to London at the weekend without thereby ceasing to be the mayor of Oberwesel. What belongs to a domain of objects is determined by specific rules or laws. Some of these rules are local and spatial. For instance, the five fingers of my left hand belong to the object domain of my left hand. If two fingers were to remain in Aarhus while I traveled to Bonn, the fingers that remained in Aarhus would very quickly cease to belong to the object domain of my left hand.

Firstly, all objects are found in object domains and, secondly, there are many object domains. Living rooms are object domains; it is to be expected that specific objects are found in them: televisions, chairs, reading lamps, coffee tables or coffee stains, etc. Likewise, galaxies are object domains; when it comes to galaxies, insofar as they are studied by astrophysics, we do not expect to come across reading lamps or coffee stains in them, but stars, planets, dark matter, black holes, and much more. Municipalities in turn house other objects: civil servants, files, laws, budgets, and boredom.

So there are many domains of objects, and under everyday conditions we are readily able to differentiate them. We know what awaits us when we enter a municipal office. We must take a small ticket, or find a place for ourselves among the mass of waiting citizens; we must wait longer at particular times than at others, and there are certain important documents that of course we have forgotten at home. However, in the object domain of a visit to such an office no physical objects in the narrow sense are to be found. The office visit concerns neither electrons nor chemical bonds. Indeed, one can analyze an office chemically or measure the precise distance between two points or the speed of determinate objects in the room (for instance, the speed of the clock hands or the rolling chairs). Still, such an investigation would be something other than an office visit. The physical or chemical analysis of a particular point in space-time taken from the office is no longer an analysis of the office, for the objects that characteristically make up an office are not found in physics or chemistry as such. This is because paper clips and civil servants are not studied in physics. Physics is concerned with movement, speed, cause and effect, statistical laws, and much more, but not civil servants or the exact number of paper clips that are used on a daily basis. For this reason one does not study literally everything in physics or chemistry. Anyone who wanted to set up a physical research project on Goethe's *Faust* would have problems applying for external funding. This is because physics is not concerned with the content of *Faust* but, at best, with the constituent objects (atoms, molecules, and so on) of the books or other documents that record the content of *Faust*.

Let us come back to our original place in the universe! We believed that our apartment was located in the universe. But that is not quite correct. For, upon closer inspection, the universe is merely the domain of objects of the natural sciences, especially of physics. Thus, we hold fast to the following: the universe is primarily something in which everything is found that is subject to experimental investigation using the methods of the natural sciences. The universe might concern four-dimensional space-time, but, since this is not completely certain, I leave the question regarding what exactly exists in the universe to the physicists. But a philosopher can judge that the universe is not everything, for it is just the domain of objects or the domain of investigation of physics. Because physics, just as every other science, is blind to everything that it does not investigate, the universe is smaller than the whole. The universe is only a part of the whole and not the whole itself.

Because the universe is the object domain of physics, with the concept "universe" we also think of the final frontier, in which we lose ourselves right away. Such infinitudes make us dizzy; we literally lose the ground beneath our feet. We only bear in mind that we stand on the earth, to which we are all gravitationally attracted by virtue of certain natural laws. The earth moves with great speed through the wide spaces of the universe without its being obvious where exactly we find ourselves. Concepts such as "center" and "periphery" are not good descriptions of space-time. For here neither the middle nor the edge exists; anyone who thinks this remains imprisoned in an ancient worldview, as if the Milky Way were in the middle and at the edge of the universe there were the risk of falling off. The pessimistic philosopher Arthur Schopenhauer once described our situation in the universe in the following way:

> In endless space countless luminous spheres, round each of which some dozen smaller illuminated ones revolve, hot at the core and covered over with a hard cold crust; on this crust a mouldy film has produced living and knowing beings; this is the empirical truth, the real, the world. Yet for a being who thinks, it is a precarious position to stand on one of those numberless spheres freely floating in boundless space, without knowing whence or whither, and to be only one of innumerable similar

beings that throng, press, and toil, restlessly arising and passing away in beginningless and endless time. Here there is nothing permanent but matter alone, and the recurrence of the same organic forms by means of certain ways and channels that inevitably exist as they do.[8]

When we place all life and all meaning in the universe, the meaning of life turns easily into the illusion, so to speak, of ants, who, despite it all, take themselves to be important. From a cosmic perspective, it looks very much as if, in the interests of pure survival, we cling to an arrogant fantasy, namely the idea that humanity and its life world are something special. But in the universe our meaning plays no central role. To a galaxy long since deceased, whose light has just reached us, it is of utterly no concern whether or not I ate breakfast this morning. In the best-case scenario, we are one biological species among others in the universe, and life is only about steering a hungry body through a material environment and cooperating with others in order to increase one's own chances of survival.

If we find no place for meaning in the universe, this is not because we are actually only ants bustling around on a lighted ball. The true ground for such an experience of insignificance and meaninglessness depends much more on the fact that we mix up completely different object domains. The universe signifies not merely a thing but also a particular kind of perspective. It is no self-evident and alternative-less location, no axiomatic name for the whole in which we find ourselves, but the result of a complex operation of thought. The universe, as large as it is, is only a part of the whole, a part to which we have access by the specific methods linked with modern science.

In a very fitting aphorism, Friedrich Nietzsche once stated the following: "Around the hero everything becomes a tragedy; around the demigod everything

becomes a satyr-play; and around God everything
becomes – what? Perhaps a world?"[9] Correspondingly
one could add that for the natural scientist everything
becomes the universe or for a soldier everything becomes
war. If one is of the opinion that all existing entities are
found in the universe, or that all events take place in the
universe, one commits the error of mistaking one object
domain among others for the whole. It would be exactly
as if one were to think that there are only plants because
one studies botany.

When we place our apartment in the universe, we
transition without noticing this from one domain of
objects to another. When we define the concept of the
universe more precisely than we usually do, it turns out
that many objects do not belong to the universe – that is,
to the object domain of the natural sciences – at all. The
television series *Stromberg* (the German version of *The
Office*) or Thomas Mann's novel *The Magic Mountain*
is not studied in any natural science, but both are nonetheless found in the object domain of living rooms. A
first conclusion from this is that there are many objects
which do not exist in the universe, a conclusion to
which one must presumably first get accustomed. Thus,
the universe is smaller than one might assume, and that
is the case even though it consists of at least hundreds of
billions of galaxies and an outrageous number of subatomic particles. It goes without saying that it is laden
with energy and facts that have not yet been fully investigated and . . . still it is only a province among others,
an ontological province among others. The universe on
that account is simply provincial, because much exists
that is not found in the universe. There are many object
domains besides the universe. This does not mean that
the other object domains exist entirely outside of the
universe, which would be a completely different (and
false) theory. Thomas Mann's *The Magic Mountain* or
the Republic of Germany do not exist in a place other

than the universe, behind or above the galaxies, as it were, and so are not "hyper"- or "meta"-galactic.

Before we can go further, it would make sense to tarry a moment with this thought in order to respond to a relevant objection. This is the claim that all the objects I have enumerated belong very well in the universe, because ultimately they all consist of matter, which is studied by physics. In principle all normal coffee tables in all normal living rooms consist of matter. However, dreamed-up coffee tables and dreamed-up living rooms, for example, do not consist of matter, just as little as imagined $100 bills consist of matter. Otherwise, by imagining $3 million, and perhaps building a beautiful town house with it, one could become rich very easily. As soon as one has paid with this imaginary money, one could restore one's imaginary bank balance just by envisaging the necessary amount. So it stands with memories. If today I remind myself five times about yesterday's dinner, I do not gain weight, because a remembered dinner – or, more exactly, the pictorial image of a dinner in one's memory – does not make one fat. The objects and scenes of memory do not exist in a material way; they are not found, or are no longer found, in the universe.

Materialism

At this point it is important to differentiate between physicalism and materialism. While PHYSICALISM claims that all existing things are located in the universe, and can for that reason be investigated physically, MATERIALISM claims that all existing things are made up of matter. Materialism in its classical variety, known since ancient Greece, claims that in truth there are only atoms and the void around them. There are indeed completely different versions of materialism, and the term can characterize completely disparate doctrines. However, here I employ it merely in the sense of two theses: firstly, everything is found in the universe and, secondly, everything that is found in the universe is material or has material foundations. All existing things, according to materialism, consist of foundational elementary particles out of which everything sticks together as in a gigantic system of Lego building blocks, from hydrogen atoms looking like the Alps to my conscious thoughts about them, which, according to materialism, are brain states and only exist as such by being material too.

Materialists assume that memories or images are as material as brain states, although the objects about which one remembers, or which one imagines, need not be material. Admittedly, that is quite remarkable. How can one explain, for example, that, although brain states are material, they are able to refer to non-material objects in the form of images? How can material objects, in any way, be about anything that is not material? When the materialist admits that brain states are about something that is not material, he has already admitted that there is something that is not material, namely all of the non-material objects brain states can be about. Let us imagine that a slimy, green, three-fingered alien is writing a book with the title *Why People Don't Exist*. As far as we know, this representation does not correspond to anything in the universe. Certainly we cannot exclude that, so that here, as in an infinite number of other cases, we can never be certain whether the content of such a brain state refers to something material or not. Even if all our thoughts could be understood as brain states and, therefore, as material, they would still be about all sorts of things that we do not believe to be material.

In addition, a second problem arises. The materialist thinks that there are non-material objects of our fantasies only because we find ourselves in certain material conditions that are about something. From this it follows that the materialist is also located in a determinate material condition whenever he thinks "There are only material conditions." We already know that some material conditions (brain states such as fantasies) refer to non-material objects, insofar as they are about them in some way. So how does the materialist know that his thought "Only material conditions exist" is not a fantasy? How can he be certain that the material conditions about which he is thinking are not fantasies and are thereby really material?

In order to make sure of this, he could proceed inductively and experimentally. For that purpose he would have to investigate all objects and all thoughts and prove that they are material. In any case that would be intricate, and for merely temporal reasons could hardly be achieved. The amount of data to be collected would be too large. One cannot verify the claim that the thought "Only material conditions exist" is true by inspecting and checking whether all objects (and therewith all thoughts) are material. Still, how does the materialist then know that all objects are material? If he cannot tell us this, we have no reason to follow materialism. Materialism is only a metaphysical assumption, only apparently better than a random worldview because it claims to be backed up by science. But it is not. Materialism is just not a claim that can be proved by natural science.

But, beyond this, it is simply false. This may be illustrated by means of two especially difficult problems for materialism. For materialism, all non-material objects exist only, as it were, as an appendage to the material. This thesis recommends itself by claiming to deliver a complete explanation of the world, which says: everything that exists is material, to which our thoughts, which are just brain states, also belong. Everything that appears as non-material is only a fantasy.

The first problem of materialism is *the problem of identification*. Materialism teaches that, in the end, my representation of a coffee table with coffee stains is reducible to the fact that the coffee table with coffee stains consists of physical objects such as subatomic particles. Yet, in order to pick correctly out of all sub-atomic particles the relevant subatomic particles for the coffee table with coffee stains – that is, to identify the right cluster of particles – it is taken for granted that we are searching for the particles of the coffee table (and not, for instance, the particles of the remote control that is lying on the coffee table). In order to do that we must recognize the existence of the coffee table, for only the coffee table leads us to its particles. The same applies to fantasies; we must recognize the existence of fantasies, and therewith non-material representational contents, in order to be able to identify the group of particles that are responsible for it. Or, more generally: materialism must recognize the existence of representations in order for it to be able to deny them at the next step. This is a contradiction.

The second quite devastating problem for material-ism consists in the idea that materialism itself is not material. Materialism is a *theory* according to which everything consists of material objects (elementary par-ticles or whatever) without exception. If this were true, then the truth of the theory of materialism would also be a configuration of elementary particles, manifest, for example, in the form of neural states of the brain of the materialist. Certainly, for an idea to be true, it is not sufficient that it is a brain state. Otherwise every thought that someone had as a brain state would be true as a result of someone having had it. The truth of the thought cannot be identical to *the fact* that someone finds herself in a determinate neurological state. Or, more generally: it is completely unclear how one should imagine a materialistic concept of truth or knowledge at all. For the truth of such a big theory as materialism is unlikely to be an elementary particle or consist of elementary particles.

Where do we stand now? We have recognized that the mental operation which places everything in the universe, from our living room, the coffee stains, our neighbors, the office employees, all the way to the galaxies, is inconsistent. Apparently one cannot place everything in the universe. This would work only if physicalism or materialism were real options. As far as both of these theories are concerned, it is a question of quite crass errors. They confuse a specific domain of objects with the whole, just as though a natural scientist told a train conductor that, in the end, he does not exist but, rather, is only a mass of particles (which, by the way, will hardly deter him from having to buy a ticket).

"The World is Everything that is the Case"

One must differentiate the world from the universe. But what is this actually, the world? What does the term "world" refer to? Nowadays we use it in everyday life, among other things, for the earth, for the planet on which we live. In English, it has become naturalized to denote more or less habitable planets, as well as those outside of our solar system, as "worlds." Moreover, there is also the use of "world" in the sense of the world of a novel, the world of the Aborigines, the world of the happy, or the world of the Romans. For starters, by nature, as it were, we tend to identify the world with the totality of all existing objects. However, in order for there to be such a totality, there must be a kind of rule or a law that holds this totality together. The world of the Romans is not simply the totality of objects that once existed in the Roman Empire, but also their relation to one another and a particular way of interacting with these objects, such as the Roman culture, its customs and practices. Ludwig Wittgenstein, in the first sentences of his *Tractatus Logico-Philosophicus*, was the first to call attention to this decisive point:

I   The world is everything that is the case.
II The world is the totality of facts, not of things.[10]

One can elucidate what is meant as follows. Let us take a well-known thing as our example: an apple. The apple is located in a fruit bowl. Let us assume that all that exists in the world is the apple, the fruit bowl, and the space which they take up. In this case, one might think that the world would be identical with the totality of the following three things:

1   the apple
2   the fruit bowl
3   the space which they take up.

Certainly this world would not be the world that it is if the apple were larger than the fruit bowl or if it were not located in the fruit bowl. For our small world consists of an apple *in* a fruit bowl. Next to the things themselves there are, therefore, facts which concern their relation to one another.

A FACT is something that is true of something. It is true of the apple that it is located in the fruit bowl. Facts are at least as important to the world as things or OBJECTS, the elements related to each other in a world. One sees this with a very simple thought experiment. Let us assume that only things exist, but no facts. In that case, nothing would be true about these things. For such truths would be facts, and we want to do without them. Consequently, in respect of these things it would be true that nothing is true about them. This is a rather obvious and objectionable contradiction. In every conceivable scenario there is at least one fact, but in some conceivable scenarios there are no things. A simple thought experiment shows that. Let us imagine that nothing existed: no space-time, no meerkats, no stockings, no planets, no suns – simply nothing at all. In this downright bleak wasteland of a situation it would be the case that nothing exists, and the thought that in this case nothing exists appears to be true. But from this it follows that in the barren nothingness there is at least one fact, namely the fact that it is a barren nothingness. This fact would in no way be nothing at all. On the contrary, it would be the all-deciding fact, the truth about the absolute desert. Accordingly, something does exist in the barren nothingness, namely that which is true about the barren nothingness. From this it follows that it is impossible that there is absolutely nothing. For there must be at least a fact in order that nothing else may be.

A world without facts does not exist. Not even nothingness can reign without there being the fact that nothing exists. When there is nothing to eat for lunch, this is a fact and, owing to the circumstances, a very annoying one. The nothingness does not exist. Always something or other is the case, always something or other is true about something or other. Nothing and no one escapes the facts. It doesn't matter how omnipotent God is, for even God could not escape the facts, since after all it would be a fact that he/she/it is God and not nothing.

A world without things is, on the contrary, easily conceivable. In my dreams there are no spatio-temporal, extended things, only dreamed-up objects (that is, as it turns out, the central difference between objects and things: the latter are always of a concrete and material nature, while the former are not unconditionally so). Dreamed-up objects are similar to spatio-temporal things, but they are not such things, for if they were it would be the case that in our dream we would step out of our body and travel around in the universe – something which I personally hold to be, well, certainly false.

We now already know that the world is at least a totality of connections. We also know that the world is the totality not only of objects or things but also of facts. At this point Wittgenstein's analysis terminates, because he was of the opinion that there is a totality of facts by virtue of which the world is defined.

But we already know more than Wittgenstein, for we already know that not only do things, objects, and facts exist, but so too do object domains. For this reason we can work with the following understanding of "the world": the world is a domain of domains, the object domain that houses all object domains (different from the universe, which accommodates only the object domain of the natural sciences). We also know that there are many object domains, which at least partly exclude one another but also partly encompass one another in different ways. The object domain of art history precludes that one chemically dissolves artworks of the Renaissance in a laboratory and puts them together again. This would annihilate the objects of art history. The object domain of whole numbers, in contrast, includes the object domain of even numbers. The object domain of local democratic politics does not allow that only a single party may run for election. It also excludes one-party systems but includes other object domains within itself, such as the resident bowling club.

Thus, the facts are not all the same. Rather, the ground of facts in object domains is divided. We still need to see whether this is actually necessary. At this point in our deliberations it is sufficient to assert that it is obvious that there are several domains of objects. Accordingly, the ground of facts has a structure that is subdivided into regions, into ONTOLOGICAL PROVINCES.

One could in turn now raise an objection. Are the object domains actually ontological provinces at the ground of facts – domains of reality, so to speak, that are differentiated from one another? Is the ground of facts really a kind of patchwork rug? Against this one might claim that the object domains with which we have occupied ourselves until now are really just different speech domains. We speak about living rooms and elementary particles, about coffee stains and local politicians, giraffes and the moon. Nevertheless, how do we know that reality or actuality itself is subdivided into these regions? Is the division of the world into object domains actually more than a *façon de parler*?

This objection could be supported by the following reflection: many objects, perhaps even all of them, are composed of other objects. My body consists of diverse organs and extremities, my books have pages, my cooker has burners, sometimes snow lies on mountain ranges, and deserts consist of innumerable grains of sand. These objects allow themselves to be rearranged differently, and their borders are often blurred. If we "cut" a new valley in the middle of a mountain range and thereby split the range, do we now have two mountain ranges or still just one (with a small gap)?

Or suppose that we enter into the workshop of an artist and see a table on which a bottle appears to stand. Because we are thirsty, we approach the table and attempt to pick up the bottle. In so doing we discover that the table and the bottle consist of a single piece which was worked on and painted by the artist, so that it appears as a wooden table on which a bottle is sitting. Such things occur even in scientific contexts. It so happens, for example, that water consists of molecules, which in turn consist of atoms, which for their part consist of nucleons. Many allegedly real object domains turn out to be illusions, merely human, all-too-human projections. With what right do we then assume that reality itself actually consists of many object domains? Are they patterns that we posit, nothing more than an expression of the human need for knowledge and error? Maybe there are absolutely no object domains but, instead, only one single totality of facts.

A whole series of inconspicuous small errors are packed into this reflection, although a few truths find expression in it. Let us begin first with the observation that we must indeed be ready under certain conditions to strike out object domains from our belief systems, a maneuver I call ONTOLOGICAL REDUCTION. One undertakes an ontological reduction when one discovers that an allegedly objective domain of discourse is – in a word – mere idle talk. In this sense, for example, everything one reads in the bull against witchcraft of Pope Innocent VIII and related texts about witches is babble, even if in the final analysis it was at that time an attempt to meet the witch nonsense with a little rationality. For this reason, one can do justice to these texts only by inquiring into the historical and psychological circumstances under which they arose. They are merely historical documents, but not documents that contain knowledge about witches. Anyone who wanted to obtain information about witches from these would be massively misguided and would be better served by *Hansel and Gretel*. The situation is similar with respect to the division of the animal and plant worlds. Biology has taught us that whales are not fish and that strawberries are not berries but belong to the accessory fruits. Much that we find out about the "world" leads us to carry out an ontological reduction, for we human beings have long found ourselves in error concerning many things. In modernity this has led to the result that, for the last five hundred years, we have trusted in the sciences to actually figure out what is the case. Because we have found out that many object domains are only empty language domains, or pure chatter, we have acquired a firm grip on the advantages of ontological reduction. "Reduction" literally means "leading back." When one carries out an ontological reduction, one leads an object domain back to a language domain and shows that the domain is not objective in the way that is insinuated but instead is determined through socio-economic or psychological contingencies. For this reason, for many object domains we need an ERROR THEORY, as it is called by philosophers. An error theory points out the systematic error of a language domain and leads this back to a series of faulty assumptions.

To carry out an ontological reduction requires substantial scientific knowledge, whether this be of a natural, historical, or sociological kind. A trailblazing Bismarck biography can change our picture of the object domain of politics just as much as someone who proves that the earth revolves around the sun and that the whole solar system, in turn, revolves around something else.

Constructivism

What all of this means is that we cannot simply ontologically reduce all of the diverse object domains to a single one. To be able to carry out a scientifically well-grounded ontological reduction of even one single object domain one must have already helped oneself to a particular scientific method. This method will be distinguished from others. For this reason one has already assumed that there are several object domains. The desire to reduce all to one is much too ambitious an undertaking that in no way accommodates the complexity of reality or the complexity of human forms of knowledge. At best, an ontological reduction of all to one is an expression of unscientific laziness.

Truly, humanity finds itself in error about quite a number of things. We cannot measure how far our ignorance extends, because in many cases we have no idea exactly what we do not know. Nevertheless, it does not follow that all object domains are only human projections, useful divisions of a homogeneous reality that, as it turns out, is largely independent of our knowledge. This is also concealed behind one of Nietzsche's famous declarations:

> No, facts is precisely what there is not, only interpretations. We cannot establish any fact "in itself": perhaps it is folly to want to do such a thing. "Everything is subjective" you say; but even this is interpretation. The "subject" is not something given, it is something added and invented and projected behind what there is.[11]

A large part of what is contained in this quotation, in which Nietzsche expresses a train of thought that even today has prominent advocates in all sciences, is false. Let us call this thought "constructivism," from which I have already distanced myself in the introduction. By CONSTRUCTIVISM I understand the assumption that "we cannot discover any fact 'in itself'" but have instead constructed all facts ourselves.

If anything at all speaks in favor of this assumption, then it is the train of thought that in fact we more or less consciously produce scientific convictions through our hardware, media, and theories: we set up experiments, formulate results with mathematical formulas and equations, dissect frogs, detect subatomic particles with the help of particular accelerators, carry out polls, compare Goethe and Schiller in dissertations, or write the history of social legislation from Bismarck until the end of the Weimar Republic.

In all these cases we make use of a particular assortment of methods and begin from particular assumptions. One can call such an assortment of premises, media, methods, and materials a REGISTRY. Every scientific investigation postulates that we help ourselves to a particular registry, by means of which we produce scientific knowledge. And, as a matter of fact, many registries would not exist if they had not been purposely devised by people. As an example, let us take a microscope by means of which we observe the bacteria *Yersinia pestis*, the cause of the plague. The technical and scientific know-how that is necessary for the construction of the microscope is immense, and the subsequent observation procedure would not have occurred without the cognitive intervention of human beings. The world domain which we observe in this way could be observed differently – with the naked eye – or we could smell the microscope or compose a poem about the fluidity that the bacteria contains; however, the result would not be the same. From this the constructivists wrongly infer that the thing which we observe – the facts – is also designed. Because the same thing can be described in different ways, and because we hold many of these descriptions to be true, they suppose that we do not "know" the facts in themselves, but only those facts which appear through the mediation of our registries. Nonetheless, because we register something differently, it does not follow that we therefore produce it.

This assumption is especially pronounced in the interpretive humanities, which have to do with cultural production and in that connection are always concerned with human, social, and historically developed constructions. For this reason, interpretations of a poem can, for example, be carried out in different registries (structural, psychoanalytic, or hermeneutic, say). Still, constructivism is not only propagated in the realm of our understanding of the interpretation of cultural productions, it also finds itself where we think of natural science as merely designing world models, instead of recognizing the physical world, the universe, as it is in itself. This picture, however, is not merely an uncalled for modesty, but actually an error which one can easily see and rectify.

Let us assume that we are currently sitting on a train and recognize that passengers are boarding. In this case it is a fact that passengers are getting on the train. Under the supposition that we are not subject to an optical illusion, which is possible but probably the exception, our registry (our eyes) conveys a true picture of the facts. The fact that we recognize exists in itself, which means, in this context, that the passengers would have got on the train even if no one on board had observed them doing so. Likewise, Goethe's Faust would have fallen in love with Gretchen even if no specialist in German studies had ever set eyes on the piece. The representation of the figure with the name "Albertine Simonet" in Proust's *In Search of Lost Time* is a complex literary engagement with the impressionism of Monet (Si-Monet), irrespective of whether or not it is discussed in an introductory course of comparative literature. The same also applies to Proust's invention of a painter named "Elstir," whom he compares with Monet in his novel. If humanity should ever forget Monet, it would still remain true that Monet lived in the same Paris as Proust – Elstir, on the contrary, only in his and our imagination. One can ask the question: Which figures or events within the world of the novel *Death in Venice* does Gustav von Aschenbach hallucinate? But that does not mean that one interprets the story correctly if one assumes that everything that Gustav von Aschenbach appears to perceive is really a hallucination and that he is actually sitting in an apartment in Hamburg, where he has taken too much LSD. This would be an odd interpretation.

Moreover, within novels, stories or films, and so on, which one commonly characterizes as "fiction," there are facts and fictions. Characters in novels can imagine states of affairs as well. Even the border between the "fictional" and "real" world, though often deemed stable, is skillfully undermined by many works of art – such as the recent genre of mockumentaries such as *The*

Office or *Parks and Recreation*. Films such as *Inception* also undermine the distinction between "fiction" and "reality." *Inception* is about a procedure that relocates us in a dream world which we take to be real, and in this way plays with the theme that films are visualized and animated dream worlds.

Whenever we recognize anything, we recognize facts. These facts are often facts in themselves, thus facts that have continued existence without us. A widespread version of constructivism today invokes brain research. One sometimes reads and hears that the colorful four-dimensional reality that we perceive is a construct or construction of our brain. In truth, according to this view, what exists are only physical particles, or some "crazy" processes, such as vibrating strings in spaces with many dimensions, or, less imaginatively, subatomic particles, which, by virtue of certain laws, coagulate, so to speak, into colorless solid bodies, off which light particles (photons) ricochet. Through contact with our nerve endings there arise impulses which our brain then unconsciously combines, as in an interactive video-game, so that we all collectively hallucinate whenever we deem to have a conscious experience of an external world consisting of green meadows, blue cubes and the like. Such "visions" are appealing, for they give our life the gloss of a science-fiction film from Hollywood and not the naked melancholy of a thinking and working animal on a ludicrously insignificant planet. Brain- or *neuroconstructivism*, as I call it, is a modern or, rather, postmodern fairytale for people who still prefer to live in a horror film such as David Cronenberg's *Videodrome* rather than in everyday life, which can at times appear somewhat trivial.

If one takes a closer look, one sees right away that, for neuroconstructivism, almost nothing is true at all, except that we have brains and that particles as well as exciting, speculative, physical theories exist. If all the things that we observe by means of our brain have absolutely nothing to do with reality, for these consist only of vibrating strings which move in eleven dimensions, then the same applies to our brain itself. Consequently, neuroconstructivism would be required to embrace its own claims, namely that we do not really have a brain. The brain qua body that we can observe by collecting data with the help of our senses would itself turn out to be a hallucination. However, from this it follows that the thesis that our colorful four-dimensional environment is only a brain simulation internal to the body is in every aspect itself only a brainless simulation. If we take neuroconstructivism at its word, we can be put at ease: for it does not exist; it is only a theory simulation and not a body of claims that is capable of being true.

The general, basic error of constructivism consists in the fact that it does not recognize that it is not a problem to recognize facts per se. The other passengers sitting next to me on the train recognize exactly the same thing as I do when they see that people are boarding the train. For these facts, it is of no concern whether it is the other passengers or I who recognize them or how we personally feel while we are observing them. We simply do not produce these facts by hallucinating them on the basis of some raw input slapping us quite literally in the face.

As we have seen, at best one can say that *some of the processes* leading to knowing are a construction: neither my neighbor on the train nor I would be in the condition to know that passengers are boarding the train if we did not have a brain or sensory receptors. But even if one claims that the process of knowing involves a construction and that, to some extent, it is adequately reconstructed by some constructivists (I would also, by the way, be in doubt about this), this does not prove that no facts exist.

In most cases the conditions of the process of knowing are to be differentiated from the conditions of the known. That I look out of the window and do not tightly close my eyes is a condition for seeing the passengers board the train. That the train has stopped and the doors have opened is, however, a condition for the passengers to board the train. The passengers do not board the train because I see them, but instead I see them because they board the train. On account of this, they do not board my consciousness or my brain, but the train.

Constructivism sometimes relies on the idea that the interpretation of what is to be interpreted (an astronomical image, a literary text, a piano sonata) is much more complex than an everyday scene at the station platform. However, the latter is also not as simple as it appears to us. No other animal on this planet is in the condition to know that passengers are boarding the train, because no other animal has the concept of trains or passengers. My dog, who is presently on the train, might be happy and wag his tail when he sees me on the platform as the doors open; however, he does not apprehend this *as* my boarding the train. Perhaps he knows that I will be with him very soon, that I wave to him, but not that the train has pulled into the station (even if he might have noticed that movement has ceased).

In the end, regarding the question of the existence of facts, it is of no consequence whether or to what extent we can know them at all. Indeed, the concept of a fact and the concept of knowledge are connected in diverse ways. Still, no analysis of this connection should lead to the false result that there exist no facts but only interpretations, and consequently the analysis, at some point, must likewise be erroneous.

Philosophers and Physicists

So far we have seen that the world itself (if it exists!) has to be divided into domains. If it were the case that it is only we who divide the world, that in itself it is not divided up, this would be like saying that in a library there are no books but only one single text. There now arises the question "Of which domains does the world consist?," which we can answer through experience and science. This is exactly what we are always trying to discover. Sometimes we are mistaken, but often we get it right.

Now we are at last equipped to answer the question "What is the world?" The world is neither the totality of things nor the totality of facts, but it is that domain in which all existing domains are found. All domains that exist belong to the world. The world is, as Martin Heidegger accurately formulated it, "the domain of all domains."[12] My view that the world does not exist accordingly amounts to the claim that there is no such thing as the domain of all domains. This leaves room for the position that there are all sorts of domains, just that they are not building blocks of a bigger, all-encompassing domain.

As I will show in the following chapters, the philosophical history of the concept of the world did not end with Heidegger. For Heidegger too at best indicated what follows from his concept of the world. Because we are concerned with knowledge of the world and its non-existence, what Heidegger actually intended naturally does not concern us. Still, we are thankful to him for the insight that the world is the domain of all domains (and, in so doing, with a friendly wave we leave him behind).

In a comment hopefully intended as a provocation (and not merely as an embarrassing demonstration of ignorance) the British physicist Stephen W. Hawking, who is highly overrated as a public intellectual, not long ago announced the following:

We each exist but for a short time, and in that time explore but a small part of the whole universe. But humans are a curious species. We wonder, we seek answers. Living in this vast world that is by turns kind and cruel, and gazing at the immense heavens above, people have always asked a multitude of questions: How can we understand the world in which we find ourselves? How does the universe behave? What is the nature of reality? Where did all this come from? Did the universe need a creator? Most of us do not spend most of our time worrying about these questions, but almost all of us worry about them some of the time. Traditionally these are questions for philosophy, but philosophy is dead. Philosophy has not kept up with the modern developments in science, particularly physics. Scientists have become the bearers of the torch of discovery in our quest for knowledge.[13]

Hawking identifies the world – the whole, the entirety or totality to which we belong – with the universe. Since time immemorial (at least since Plato and Aristotle) philosophy has distinguished between the universe, in the sense of the domain of objects studied by physics, and that which we moderns call "the world." And we already know that the universe is an ontological province, something that has not occurred to Hawking because, for him (as a physicist), everything becomes physics. Had he known anything about philosophy and its history, he would have noticed that for a considerable time philosophers have argued that precisely the questions he himself raises cannot be answered by finding out more about the universe.

Of course one can criticize philosophy for having not yet sufficiently developed the concept of the world. The reason for this lies in the fact that for ages philosophers have allowed themselves to be overawed, so to speak, by modern natural science. Among influential contemporary German philosophers this applies even to Jürgen Habermas. Habermas adopts, with a few modifications, Kant's concept of the world. To put it briefly, Kant says, and with him Habermas, that the world is a "regulative idea." This means that we presuppose a world whole, and that everything we experience and know must be understood as a section of the world whole. In this way we guarantee that we can have a coherent and contradiction-free picture of the world, for the world itself is a unity whose sections we are able to represent. Habermas's point is that the world in this sense, of course, is not a thing, nor can it be identical with the universe. In this model the world itself is not found as a section of the world; rather, it is only an idea which we presuppose in order to be able to make the sections intelligible. Habermas explicitly calls this a "formal-pragmatic presupposition of the world,"[14] and in the end he connects this to our knowledge of the world, which is always realized by our communicative practices:

> A shared view of reality as a "territory halfway between" the "world views" of different languages is a necessary presupposition of meaningful dialogue *überhaupt*. For the interlocutors, the concept of reality is connected with the regulative idea of a "sum total of all that is knowable."[15]

In another place Habermas speaks of the "totality of objects,"[16] which we already know is a false concept of the world. Habermas is unfortunately content to reserve a small area of language and discourse analysis for philosophy and surrenders the remainder of knowledge of actuality to the natural and social sciences.[17] In the process he fails to justify his own concept of the world, because first and foremost it is convenient for him to defend the domain of the social world as a region of analysis for philosophy. Nonetheless, we have already seen how the thesis that the world is the "totality of objects" or the "entirety of entities" is false. If the world were the totality of objects and nothing further, no facts would exist.

In addition, the other definition that Habermas employs, namely "the sum of everything knowable," does not lead much further. For not all facts are knowable – in any case, not for people. For example, consider the internal conditions of a black hole. The conditions in its immediate environment are incompatible with our capacity to know what exactly happens in it (granted that anything happens there at all). From this it does not follow that there are no facts inside of the black hole, but only that many, if not all of them, are not knowable in any sense that is intelligible to us.

Another example is provided by actively withdrawing objects – objects that disappear whenever one observes them.[18] For instance, it could be the case that pink elephants, made of a heretofore unknown material, are hidden on the far side of the moon. Whenever we are successful in observing the far side of the moon, the elephants withdraw by traveling to another place with the speed of light or by disguising themselves as moon craters. Quite a few interpreters of Heisenberg's famous uncertainty principle understand some properties of particles as partially actively withdrawing objects. For, by virtue of our measuring, we change the properties of the particles in such a way that we cannot exactly measure other properties at the same time. This simply depends upon the fact that every observation (also those with our sense organs) and every measurement procedure is itself a physical intervention in the physical environment.

From these reasons, which have only been touched on and ought to be more fully developed, it follows that Habermas's concept of the world is verifiably false. While Hawking underestimates philosophy because he does not have any adequate representation regarding that with which philosophy is concerned, Habermas is too modest and cautious because he does not wish to raise any premature objections against the results of scientific research. Yet Habermas overestimates and asks too much of the natural sciences. Even if it is in principle commendable to insist on science, reason, and enlightenment, still one should not without reason thereby disparage philosophical science. It progresses and regresses like the other sciences. A great advance of philosophy is its improvement of the concept of the world, which Habermas does not sufficiently bring into account and about which Hawking does not have the slightest clue.[19] One does not establish the case that philosophy is dead by knowing nothing about it or its history, just as one does not kill everybody one does not know.

Let us summarize the five most important results of these first chapters.

1 The universe is the object domain of physics.
2 There are many object domains.
3 The universe is one among many object domains (even if it is an impressively large one) and for this reason it is an ontological province.
4 Many object domains are also domains of discourse. Perhaps surprisingly, some object domains are actually only domains of discourse (mere chatter).
5 The world is neither the entirety of objects or things nor the entirety of facts. It is the domain of all domains.

II

What is Existence?

We have already seen that there exist completely different things and object domains: meerkats, local elections, the universe, and living rooms. Besides this, we have already recognized what things, object domains, and facts are. In this chapter we will devote ourselves to fields of sense. I will argue for the thesis that FIELDS OF SENSE are the relevant ontological elements – they are the places where everything appears. My answer to the question "What is existence?" is as follows: existence is the circumstance that something appears in a field of sense.

One can again easily approach this thought in an intuitive way. Let us think about a rhinoceros in a field. This rhinoceros exists. After all, it stands in the field. The circumstance that it stands in the field, that it belongs to the field of sense of the field, is its existence. Existence is thereby to be found not immediately in the world but in one of its domains. In this chapter you will learn why these domains are fields of sense and what this means.

Let us come back to ONTOLOGY. By this term I understand the systematic answer to the question "What is existence?" and what the term "existence" means. I differentiate this from metaphysics. By METAPHYSICS I understand the systematic answer to the question

"What is the world?" and what the term "world" means. Metaphysics usually assumes the existence of the world.

So, let us begin with ontology. When I say that the answer must be "systematic," I mean only that we employ considerations in which the principles and thought trains that we establish and justify are connected with one another and make up a single body of thought, a theory. In contrast to other sciences, the material of ontology consists of concepts we analyze. Whether the analysis is successful depends upon many factors. In particular, ontology must remain in contact with our experience of reality. When we come upon a claim that cannot be brought into accord with any of our experiences in any way, we must have committed a mistake, for we want to explain what it means for something to exist. And we have some understanding of what this means. If our explanation suddenly rules out the existence of something that obviously exists, we must inquire into what has gone wrong. Some ontologists have claimed, for example, that nothing at all exists, that nothing moves, or that the flow of time is only an illusion. Others think that neither the past nor the future exists but only the present (and not even this exactly). Others again are of the opinion that there are innumerable possible worlds besides ours, with which we cannot come into physical contact. All of these odd suppositions result from a false ontology.

When one honestly gets the idea that time does not pass while one is formulating one's ontology, something has obviously gone wrong. Besides this, I am certain that during the composition of these lines a number of things have moved: my finger, the cursor, my mouse, my eyes, parts of my brain, my muscles, my heart, or the train in which I am sitting. We ought to proceed with caution in the first steps of ontology and not risk any large leaps.

For this reason, let us begin with a very simple

observation! All objects with which we are concerned have specific properties. My dog has (luckily) four legs, has a coat that is variously white, brown and grey, is called "Havannah," is smaller than I am, likes yoghurt, and has a specific genetic code. In comparison to this, Leo the lion (if he even exists) lives in South Africa, has a powerful mane, would be in the condition to devour my dog in one bite, has a different genetic code, successfully hunts gazelles, and never has a bath (well, you could certainly give it a try!). Besides Havannah and Leo there are many other objects with completely different properties: black holes, David Lynch films, and sad thoughts at the beginning of winter, as well as the Pythagorean theorem. All of these objects have specific properties that differentiate them from other objects in their physical, emotional, or logical environment.

Or the other way around: what distinguishes objects and domains of objects from one another are the properties that are attributed to them. The domain of objects of whole numbers is differentiated from Leo insofar as it is not a living creature, that it contains more numbers than Leo has teeth, or that it can be described with true sentences in various mathematical systems. My sad thoughts at the beginning of winter are also explicitly differentiated from whole numbers through their properties. I do not thereby mean to exclude the possibility that one or another elementary school child has sad thoughts at the beginning of winter on account of whole numbers.

Properties distinguish objects in the world from several other objects in the world. This immediately provides the opportunity to ask at least two philosophical questions that form the core of my considerations:

1 Can an object exist which has all of the properties there are?
2 Are all objects differentiated from all other objects?

I answer both questions with "no." From this I will infer that the world does not exist. For, firstly, the world would be the object which has all properties and, secondly, in it all objects would have to be differentiated from all other objects. Let us proceed systematically step by step and begin with question number 1.

The Super-Object

Objects are those things about which we can reflect with thoughts that are apt to be true. By that I mean the following: a thought that is apt to be true is a thought that can be true or false. This does not apply to all thoughts. Let us take the thought

So what?

The thought "So what?" is not apt to be true, for it is neither true nor false. It is different from the thought

There are weapons of mass destruction in Luxembourg.

At a specific time this thought is obviously either true or false. On the spur of the moment I deem it to be false, but I do admit that I could be wrong. There are, however, many thoughts which are not apt to be true, for example

Mumble, mumble

or

Sweden, Sweden, every mountain.

Many thoughts which run through our consciousness are quite incomplete formations. Sometimes we just begin with a thought and then suddenly turn our attention to another before the first has even become truth apt. We do not constantly think in complete, well-formulated sentences or in ways that could contribute towards the formation of a theory. However, it is important to keep the following distinction in mind. The thought

It is raining right now in London

is capable of being true. What's more, I can easily check it by googling the weather in London or by calling someone in the city and inquiring whether it is raining there right now. The thought

Exactly 3 million years ago the number of galaxies in the universe was odd

is also capable of being true but is just very difficult, or perhaps not even possible, to verify. The scope of thoughts which are verifiable by human beings is much smaller than the scope of objects and facts themselves. The thoughts that are verifiable by us are, so to speak, a small bright region of the whole that Martin Heidegger described with a famous metaphor as "the clearing." We stand in a clearing in the middle of a forest, or rather in a quite large jungle, that we cannot survey completely.

Compared to the unsurveyable domains in which we happen to find ourselves, what appears in the cone of light of human knowledge is insignificant, even if it is of utmost importance to human beings. So, let us ignore everything that is found somewhere in the jungle outside of the clearing, and let us limit ourselves to what is knowable. If we know something about an object, we know some of its properties. By virtue of these properties the object stands out among other objects. The idea of existence comes from the Latin (with an ancient Greek pre-history). The word "existere" means "to originate," "to come forward." Translated literally, it means "to stand out," "to stick out," or "to step out."* What exists sticks out; it sets itself apart from other objects by virtue of its properties.

When we recognize all the properties of an object, we recognize the whole object. Once again, an object is not something in addition to its properties, as this would be just another of its properties. I am all of my properties; you are all of your properties. If, on top of all of that, I were also the bearer of my properties, this would simply add to the stock of my properties.

An object that would have all possible properties – let us call it the SUPER-OBJECT – cannot exist, however, or stand out against the mass of other objects. The reason for this is easy to see: the super-object would have all the other objects in itself; it would encompass all other objects, and so it could not emerge out of them or stick out among them. It could also not stick out against a background, as it would have to encompass any possible background within itself. Ordinary objects are describable by virtue of a finite and limited stock of properties. Our dog has four legs, has a coat that is variously white, brown and grey, and is of a particular size. But he is not Batman. Something that is distinguished from all other things just by itself, by virtue of nothing more than that, and is identical only to itself, cannot exist. It ceases to come forward. Just try to imagine everything, absolutely everything, in one stroke. You will soon find that you always assume a background against which the super-object stands out – such as your own thought or your own consciousness of it.

* In the original German, Gabriel identifies "existere" as "entstehen," "heraustreten," and points out that it may be literally translated as "heraus-stehen" (to stand out), "hervorstechen" (to stick out), or "hervortreten" (to step out).

Monism, Dualism, Pluralism

The idea that a super-object exists has been quite widely promulgated for millennia. Even in contemporary philosophy it has many followers – for example, the American philosopher Terence E. Horgan, who, with reference to the science-fiction classic *The Blob* and its 1998 remake, designated the super-object as the "Blobject."[20] His thesis of BLOBJECTIVISM claims that there is only a single all-encompassing domain of objects and assumes that this object domain is itself an object. In this model all properties would be combined into a single domain that could itself become the object of our metaphysical contemplation. Now, if one understands this object as the bearer of all possible properties, or at least of all properties ever realized, one has introduced the super-object.

Philosophers traditionally call the bearers of properties SUBSTANCES. Here, one should not imagine any concrete material substances in the everyday, ordinary sense of "stuff." Since the onset of modernity, with its great metaphysicians René Descartes, Georg Wilhelm Leibniz and Baruch Spinoza, there has been an ongoing dispute about how many substances actually exist. Above all, there are three theses in the running. These are still heavily discussed and have sharp-witted followers.

1   MONISM (Spinoza) Only one single substance exists, the super-object.
2   DUALISM (Descartes) Two substances exist – thinking substance (*substantia cogitans*) and extended, material substance (*substantia extensa*). Dualists believe that the human mind is of a completely different nature than the human body. In this context, they typically promote the notion that the thinking substance can actually exist independently of the material body, while some assume that there is no

immortal thinking soul, but only two substances which are connected with each other.

3 PLURALISM (Leibniz) Many substances exist. Strictly speaking, pluralism is even committed to the thesis that infinitely many substances exist. Leibniz named these substances "monads." A MONAD is a maximally self-sufficient object which is completely independent of all other objects by having a determinate and limited number of properties.

My own position is a form of pluralism, and I am convinced that monism as well as dualism are demonstrably false. Monism is refuted by the proof that there is no world, which will be made clear after the next chapter at the latest. Dualism is much easier to refute, for even at a cursory glance it is absurd. If one assumes two substances, how does one know that there are not more than two? Why two and not twenty-two?

The question "How many substances actually exist?" is more exciting than it may appear at first glance. Let us take a closer look! There are individual objects such as handbags and crocodiles. These objects are constituted in turn by other objects – handbags, for example, are occasionally made up of crocodile leather, and crocodiles (more uncommonly) are even made up of handbags (when, for example, they have just devoured a woman with a handbag). Many individual objects consist of other individual objects. There is actually a separate subdomain of logic which busies itself with formal relations of parts and wholes: MEREOLOGY (from Greek "to meros" = "part").

Handbags and crocodiles are differentiated in such a way that they seldom take up the same space. In that way they are divided; each concerns different individual objects. This also applies to my left and my right hand. Nevertheless, my left hand and my right hand belong together, for they are parts of my body. Thus, we have the case of two spatially separated, individual objects (handbags and crocodiles) and the case of two individual objects that are likewise spatially separated, but which are connected by virtue of one whole of which they are part (my left and my right hand).

There is at least a third case. Towards this end, let us think about a cordless phone. When we buy a cordless phone, we acquire a receiver and a part that is separable from the receiver, the handset. In this case we have two individual objects (a receiver and a handset) which make up a single object (the cordless phone) without their having to be spatially connected all the time. This also applies to the USA: Alaska or Hawaii are not spatially bound to the other states. Of course, the same applies to Heligoland and Bavaria: both are parts of Germany, even though they are not spatially bound in the same landmass, although Bavaria is spatially more closely linked to the rest of Germany than Heligoland. Now Hawaii and Heligoland are objects completely in their own right. One can view them independently of their membership in the state – something which is only conditionally the case in respect to my left hand because, after all, as my left hand it belongs to the whole, my body. Also, the mereological connection between the receiver and the handset is closer than that between Hawaii and Heligoland.

Receiver and handset form a MEREOLOGICAL SUM which makes up a completely different individual object, the cordless phone. Thus the following mereological equation is true: receiver + handset = cordless phone. The same does not apply when I put the handset in my left hand: the mereological sum "left hand + handset" does not form a genuine individual object such as a "left-handset." There are simply no left-handsets, but on the other hand there are definitely cordless phones.

Thus, not all objects we bind together in some way form a new, complex object. For this reason the following question can be raised: "In which cases do we form, justifiably and with objective grounds, new objects?" Considered in the abstract, one might be of the opinion that each random object can be joined with every other random object to form a whole. Let us take my nose and my left ear. Is there really a mereological sum consisting of my nose and my left ear, my left "near," so to speak? Obviously we distinguish between real mereological sums and mere aggregates or heaps of objects. Not every heap of objects is an actual individual object. Still, according to what criterion do we decide under what conditions something is a real mereological sum?

When I shake your hand, do we thereby melt into one person? Obviously not, although we form a spatial unity. Thus, the unity of persons cannot consist exclusively in the formation of a spatial unity. In respect to other objects – mountains, for instance – it appears that spatial proximity is enough in order to form a new object – a mountain range. Nevertheless, which criteria do we apply in order to differentiate actual mereological sums from heaps of properties or objects? I am of the opinion that there is no available catalogue of criteria independent of experience by means of which we divide the world into real mereological sums. We sometimes even divide the world falsely – whenever we take whales to be fish, for example. There is simply no algorithm by means of which one could write a program that determines for every conglomeration of properties whether there is an actual mereological sum coordinated with it. There are various catalogues of criteria, and some of these categories prove themselves over time to be false.

With this background in mind, let us return to our leading question – whether or not there is a super-object. If there were a super-object, it would be the mereological sum of all properties – a strange thought! For one could establish the mereological sum of all properties without any criterion. Every property belongs to this sum, independently of which criterion we apply. An object, something about which we learn something without applying any criterion, and to which we simply assign any and every arbitrary property, would be a very remarkable thing, for it would be composed of my left hand, Angela Merkel's favorite book, and the most expensive Currywurst south of Frankfurt. To search for an object about which one can assert with a true statement that it is everything – my left hand, Angela Merkel's favorite book and the most expensive Currywurst south of Frankfurt, plus everything else – would in any case be an extremely extravagant research project.

The reason for this lies in the fact that an object which has all properties exists only apparently, as if it were the biggest heap of stuff, a conglomeration of what there is which we can select without any more specific criterion. The word "criterion" comes from the ancient Greek verb "krinein," which means "differentiating" and in philosophy also means "judgment,"* a stem that also hides behind the word "crisis." Criteria correspond to differences which are adequate to a determinate object or object domain. Where no criterion is available, no determinate objects or even indeterminate objects exist. For even indeterminate or relatively indeterminate objects (such as a heap of rice, for example, which one may serve for dinner) are determined by somewhat looser criteria and must be differentiated from other objects.

Thus, it is false that there exists only one substance – a super-object – which has all properties. Monism is false; it is actually necessarily false, since the concept of the super-object is incoherent. Dualism, on the other hand, is indeed capable of truth, but completely unjus-

---

* In German "judgment" is "Urteil." Translated quite literally, it means "the original [Ur] division [Teil]." As the "original division," the connection to differentiation is more obvious than the English term "judgment."

tified. Why should there only be these two substances, and in particular exactly these two substances now made famous by Descartes?

Only a very superficial observation speaks in favor of Cartesian dualism, namely the notion that there is a difference between thoughts and those things with which thoughts are concerned. When I think that it snows, it is not snowing in my thoughts, for one would otherwise have to say that my thoughts have a climate, and that it is winter there or that I have frozen water in my thoughts. Then I could, for instance, thaw my thoughts and drink the fresh water. This would simplify a trip through the desert, because one could simply drink one's thoughts about cool water. The thought about snow and snow itself simply belong to two different domains of objects. Now, Descartes falsely thinks that it is enough to divide the world into these two domains on the basis of that difference. At best, it amounts to an insight into there being two substances, which leaves it completely open as to whether or not there might not be many more.

Monism is false, and dualism is unjustified. On account of this, by virtue of a simple process of elimination, only pluralism is left, which, however, we must radically modernize.

Absolute and Relative Differences

Let us come back to the question that we raised above. Are all objects differentiated from all other objects? At first glance this appears to be the case. Every object appears to be identical to itself and different from all other objects. Yes, my left hand is my left hand (not very informative, but true) and is not my right hand (also not very informative, but still true).

However, this train of thought is full of errors and

trapdoors which can once again easily be overlooked. Let us imagine that we know that some object G exists. At first we do not know any more than that. Now we ask someone, who is familiar with G, whether G is a screen, to which he answers in the negative. "Is G a rhinoceros?" "No." "Is G a red can?" "No." "Is G a material object?" "No." "Is G an immaterial object?" "No." "Is G a number?" "No." This dialogue would be just as in the game "Who am I?," in which each of us in turn sticks the name of a famous person or object on our foreheads and tries to figure out who or what we are.

Let us assume that we had a lot of time and listed all the other objects besides G, and we would only ever discover from the expert that G is not identical to these. In this case G would be identical to itself exactly insofar as it is differentiated from all other objects. Still, if this were the case, G would no longer have any core: G would be only negatively determined such that G is not everything else. We would thereby know nothing positive about G. If we want to know what G is, we would have to know something else about it besides the claim that it is not identical with any other object. It follows that the identity of G cannot be identical to the difference between G and all other objects. Expressed again in very simple terms: G must have some property of its own that consists of more than its difference from all other objects. The property that an object is identical to itself is terribly uninteresting and unhelpful.

We can radicalize this idea: suppose that we did not know a single object (besides the expert himself) and asked him what each object was but only ever learned that it is not all other objects (which we do not yet know). In this way we could never obtain the slightest positive information about any object whatsoever.

Nevertheless, it is pertinent that we fix the identity of an object, among other things, by giving an account of its difference from other objects. Yet this never amounts to an absolute difference. An ABSOLUTE DIFFERENCE – a difference between an object and all other objects – is uninformative, for it claims only that an object is not identical with any other but identical with itself alone, which contains no information. What differentiates objects from one another has to be a more informative criterion. To know what differentiates one object from another consists in our having information about the object. An uninformative difference is thus no difference. For this reason we must differentiate between an absolute difference (which is senseless and uninformative) and a relative difference. A RELATIVE DIFFERENCE is a difference between an object and several other objects.

A relative difference consists in an informational contrast. Informational contrasts, in turn, are found in completely different shades. Coca-Cola contrasts with Pepsi, beer, wine, ice pop, and many other things. But Coca-Cola does not contrast with rhinoceros. Therefore no one would say to a waiter: "Please bring me a Coca-Cola or, if you don't have Coca-Cola, a rhinoceros will do!" The reason that we never think about whether we would prefer to have a cola or a rhinoceros, plain and simple, is because cola does not contrast with rhinoceros.

At this point we will try out a little sleight of hand in order to clarify the difference between relative and absolute difference. Is it not the case that the rhinoceros contrasts with the rest of the world? Whenever we turn our attention to the rhinoceros, do we not turn it away from the rest of the world? This is not the case for a variety of reasons: when we turn our attention to the rhinoceros, we have already placed it in an environment, for example in a zoo or a television show. It is simply impossible to be attentive to a rhinoceros independently of its environment. The French philosopher Jacques Derrida expressed this with his phrase "there is nothing outside of the text,"[21] which has been misunderstood by many (and intentionally formulated in an unclear way). We can therefore put it in a less postmodern fashion: rhinos are always found in some environment or other. Of course Derrida did not want to say that, in reality, rhinos are texts; rather, only that neither rhinos nor anything else exist independently of contexts.

But can one not simply differentiate the rhinoceros in its environment from the rest of the world? This also leads no further, because once again one needs an environment for the environment. For environments too are found only in environments. An absolute contrast always carries too large a contrast with itself. A contrast that is too large leads to our inability to know anything.

This is not only a fact about the limits of human knowledge. This applies much more to the information that we gather. Reality itself makes information available – for example, the information that there is only a single moon. This information does not come into the world through human beings differentiating heavenly bodies from one another. The difference between the sun, the earth and the moon is no human doing but a condition for the existence of knowing beings and intelligent life on our planet.

Thus, no absolute difference exists. Some things are differentiated from some other things. But it is not the case that everything is differentiated from everything else. Some things are actually identical with some other things, something that poses a well-known philosophical riddle: How can two different objects or facts be identical with each other? This must be possible, for the Rhine is identical to itself, although it is constantly changing. The material out of which the Rhine consists today is constantly being replaced, and the river does not remain the same over time. At this point, let's go on the record: objects are always differentiated from other objects. There are contrast classes, which are always relative and never absolute. We are sometimes mistaken about the determination of the relevant contrast classes, from which, however, it does not follow that there are no contrast classes at all. Quite to the contrary: we are sometimes mistaken about the determination of the relevant contrast classes because contrast classes, about which we are mistaken, really exist.

Fields of Sense

My own answer to the question "What is existence?" boils down to the claim that, although *the* world does not exist, there do exist *infinitely many* worlds, which in part overlap but are also partly independent of one another. However, the term "world" is deceptive, as it always suggests some kind of closed totality. This is why the formulation that there are infinitely many worlds should be replaced by a different version, one which does not make use of the misleading idea that there could be a world – albeit only in the plural. We already know that the world is the domain of all domains and that existence has something to do with something being found in the world. But this means that something is found in the world only if it is found in a domain. From this I infer that we must somewhat improve the equation

existence = being found in the world

if it is already pointing us in the right direction. Here is my own equation:

existence = appearing in a field of sense.

This equation is the basic principle of fields of sense ontology. It results from accepting that to exist is to be found in a world (a field of sense) while giving up on the mistaken idea that there has to be an all-encompassing field of sense (the world writ large). The ONTOLOGY OF FIELDS OF SENSE claims that, whenever a field of sense can be found in which it appears, there is something rather than nothing. APPEARANCE is a general name for "to be found in" or "occurrence."* The concept of appearance is just more neutral. What is false also appears even if it goes against the ordinary use of speech to say that what is false is found in the world. Furthermore, "occurrences" are more concrete than "appearances," on account of which I prefer the more flexible concept of appearance. Note: that something appears false (and thereby exists) does not mean that it is true. Appearance/existence is not identical with truth. It is indeed true that it is false that witches exist. Witches appear in the false thought that they exist in Northern Europe. False thoughts exist, but the objects they are about are not found in the field in which false thoughts place them.

We now know approximately what an appearance is. But what is a field of sense? We have already spoken about objects: local politics, art history, physics, living

---

* The German "Vorkommen" is here translated as "to be found in" and "Vorkommnis" as "occurrence." "Vorkommen" has many meanings. Literally, it signifies that which "comes" (kommen) "forth" (vor). It can signify "to appear" or "to seem," as in "es kommt mir so vor" (it seems to me). The term "appear" has been reserved for "Erscheinung" in order to keep important terminology constant. "Vorkommen" can also be used to signify that something is found in a particular environment. For example, one might say that "Kühe kommen nicht im Dschungel vor" – i.e., "cows are not found in the jungle." This sense of "Vorkommen" most closely expresses Gabriel's meaning: objects are "found in" or "take place" in fields of sense. Naturally, this does not mean that their existence depends upon their being discovered. It simply means that the object "occurs" or "takes place" in a field of sense or in an environment. One should not think that Gabriel is privileging events because of the use of "occurrence." It is meant to signify that something takes place somewhere and does not privilege the category of "event."

rooms, and so on. When we understand these objects as objects, we tend (even if it is not necessary) to abstract from how the objects appear in domains. How objects appear often has something to do with their specific qualities. It appertains to works of art that they appear to us in various ways. But it does not appertain to nucleons that they appear to us in various ways. One is not able to interpret them in different ways; rather, one only understands what they are in themselves if one is proficient in a domain of objects in which they are found. Fields of sense can be vague, colorful and relatively indeterminate; domains of objects consist of numerable objects which are distinctly differentiated from one another. For fields of sense this is not unconditionally the case. These can contain iridescent, ambivalent appearances.

At this point the logician and mathematician Gottlob Frege, who wrote a few very influential philosophical papers, can be of additional help, for during Frege's time the discussion of object domains had already become established; it also played an important role in the development of modern logic, which, however, advances quite a false concept of existence. Readers who have not busied themselves with modern logic may be amazed that modern logicians think that existence is always countable – a fallacious and distorted claim. When I wonder whether there are horses, I do not wonder *how many* horses exist, but *whether* horses exist. One should differentiate the interrogative words "how many" and "whether."

Modern logic has almost completely conflated the concept of the object domain with the concept of quantity. However, not all domains are quantities of countable and mathematically describable objects, since this does not apply to works of art or complex feelings. Not all domains in which something appears are object domains in that sense. Thus the more general concept is the concept of the field of sense. Fields of sense can indeed present themselves as domains of objects in the sense of countable objects or in a more precise sense of mathematically countable quantities. They can just as well be composed of iridescent appearances, something that does not apply either to domains of objects or to quantities in general.

The mistaken development in modern logic, namely the confusion between existence and being countable (a typical mistake which happens if one wants to count and calculate everything), overlooks a groundbreaking hint of Frege's that will help us further. Let us return to identity. In a little masterpiece, his essay "On Sense and Reference," Frege asked the question "How can propositions of identity be both consistent and informative?"[22] Let us take the proposition:

> The actor who was Hercules in New York is identical to the thirty-ninth governor of California.

Normally one would not formulate this proposition in such a complicated way. In a biography of Arnold Schwarzenegger it might read thus:

> Hercules in New York later became the thirty-ninth governor of California.

Another simple example of an identity statement is:

$$2 + 2 = 3 + 1$$

It is not a contradiction that Arnold Schwarzenegger was Hercules in New York at one time and governor of California at another. Both are correct. The same applies to the number 4. It can be written as $2 + 2$ as well as $3 + 1$ (and in endless other ways).

Now Frege calls "$2 + 2$" and "$3 + 1$" "modes of presentation" and makes this synonymous with the term "sense."[23] The sense of terms identified in an identity statement is diverse, though that to which they refer is identical (for example, Arnold Schwarzenegger or the number 4). Thus, from a true, informative, and consistent proposition of identity we learn that the same thing (the same person, the same fact) can be presented in different ways. Instead of speaking of "presentation," I prefer the word "appearance." A SENSE is then the way in which an object appears.

Fields of sense are domains in which something – a determinate object – appears in a certain way. When one considers object domains and *a fortiori* quantities, one abstracts from fields of sense. In this way, two fields of sense can refer to the same objects, which nonetheless appear differently in both fields of sense. Here is a fitting example.

Let us consult what is by now a familiar object: my left hand. (You can also use your own left hand for the following experiment. Philosophical experiments are extremely cheap and easy to conduct without a lab.) My left hand is a hand. It has five fingers, is presently far from tanned, and has fingertips and grooves in the palm. What appears to me as my left hand is nonetheless a conglomeration of elementary particles, let us say a determinate whirl of atoms, which are themselves a whirl of still smaller particles. But it could also appear to me as a work of art, or as a tool with which I carry my lunch to my mouth. Here is another example that comes from Frege: there may be a grove in a forest, or there might simply be five individual trees that are part of the forest. The same thing can be a grove (one sense) or five trees (another sense). Depending on the field of sense, the same thing is a hand, a whirl of atoms, a work of art, or a tool. And the five trees are a grove or individual trees (or again: another whirl of atoms).

Gustav von Aschenbach is a character invented by

Thomas Mann as well as a pedophile, but he is not a whirl of atoms in our universe, because there never existed in the universe a whirl of atoms that was identical to the person named "Gustav von Aschenbach" invented by Mann. Depending on the field of sense, Gustav von Aschenbach was either in Venice or he was not. It depends on whether one is talking about the novel or the history of the city located in a specific region on our planet.

There are no objects or facts outside of fields of sense. Everything that exists appears in a field of sense (strictly speaking, it actually appears in an infinite number). "Existence" means that something appears in a field of sense. An infinite number of things appear in a field of sense without anyone ever having noticed this at any time. From an ontological point of view, it does not matter whether we human beings have been informed about this or not. Things and objects do not appear because they appear to us; they do not exist only because this has occurred to us. Most things simply appear without our taking notice of them. One should never forget this, for fear of becoming the Baccalaureus from Goethe's *Faust II*, who in the play is seduced into constructivism by Mephistopheles, the devil. Goethe, for whom constructivism, which first originated with Kant, was a lifelong annoyance in all of its variations, lets the Baccalaureus character declaim the following:

The World was not until I made it be;
I guided the sun from out the sea;
The moon began her changing course with me;
And lo! The day adorned itself to meet me,
The earth turned green and blossomed forth to greet me.
I beckoned, and upon that earliest night
The firmament made all its splendors bright.
Who, tell me, if not I, freed all you thinkers
From narrow philistines' confining blinkers?

But I, true to my spirit's dictates, free,
In joy pursue the flame that burns in me,
And pace along, entranced with my own kind,
The light before me, darkness left behind.[24]

Our planet is not the center of cosmological and ontological events but, at the end of the day, an infinitesimally small corner in which we have to some degree made ourselves at home and which we instantly destroy, because we overestimate our importance in the universe. Insofar as we believe that the world would not exist without us, we might also erroneously think that the universe will care whether human beings continue to exist. Unfortunately it is not so simple. Neither the universe nor space-time is interested in the fact that there are beings such as ourselves on this beautiful planet. Seen in light of the whole, it doesn't really matter whether we exist and what pride we take in our existence. To this day, this insight is actually downplayed in the academic community, and many philosophers, as well as physicists, think that the universe is concerned with us. We will come to discuss this situation later in connection with religion, when we reach a point where we can cautiously approach the term "God." However, it follows that, by and large, it doesn't really matter whether humans exist – not that it doesn't matter to you or to me. One should not confuse the world with the world of the human being and one should not set it up on the wrong level.

All things appear in fields of sense. EXISTENCE is a property of fields of sense, namely that something appears in them. I claim that existence is not a property of objects in the world or in fields of sense, but a property of fields of sense, namely the property that something appears in them. Yet does this not yield the following problem? Fields of sense are objects, for we think about them with truth-apt thoughts. When they have the property that something appears in them, does existence not in this respect become a property of objects? But, if fields of sense appear in fields of sense (otherwise they could not exist), I appear to have contradicted myself. However, this contradiction does not follow because the world does not exist at all. There are infinitely many fields of sense which partly overlap each other, and on another level just never come into contact. As Peter Emptiness in Pelevin's novel noted: in the end everything takes place nowhere. But this does not mean that nothing at all takes place, but the opposite, that infinitely many things happen – they are just not coordinated by appearing in an all-encompassing field of sense. We willingly overlook this, because we cannot attend to an infinite number of things at once.

III

Why the World Does Not Exist

First and foremost let us seize upon our first great piece of knowledge, the principle of fields of sense:

existence = appearance in a field of sense.

In order for something to be able to exist it must belong to a field of sense. Water can belong in a bottle, a thought belongs in my worldview, as citizens human beings can belong to states, the number 3 belongs among the whole numbers, and molecules belong among the universe. How something belongs to a field of sense is just how it appears. It is pivotal that the way in which a thing appears is not always identical. Not everything appears in the same way, and not everything belongs to a field of sense in the same way.

Given that all of this is the case, we can now pose the question "Does the world exist?" – "Is there a world?" We saw in the first chapter that at best one can conceive the world as the domain of all domains. This conception, which goes back to Heidegger, we can once again clarify by saying that the world is the field of sense of all fields of sense, that field of sense in which all other fields of sense appear, and for this reason it is the domain to which everything belongs. This is, so to speak, my last word concerning the world, so that it is italicized and belongs in the glossary: *the* WORLD *is the field of sense in which all other fields of sense appear.*

Against this background it is altogether tempting to believe that everything that there is exists in the world, because the world is simply the domain in which everything takes place. And, certainly, nothing exists outside of the world. Everything that one takes to be external to the world therefore belongs to the world. Existence always contains a specification of place. Existence means that something appears in a field of sense. Thus, if the world exists, the question is: "In which field of sense does it exist?" Let us take for granted that the world exists in field of sense (S1). (S1) is in this case one field of sense among others; besides (S1) there are also (S2), (S3), and so on. If the world appears in (S1), which exists among other fields of sense, the world itself exists. Is that possible?

The world is the field of sense in which all fields of sense appear. Accordingly every other field of sense appears as a subfield of (S1). For the world appears in (S1), and everything appears in the world.

Thus, (S2), (S3), and so on do not appear *next to* (S1), but they also appear *in* (S1), because the world appears in (S1), in which, according to its definition, everything appears. Thus (S2) exists twice: once *next to* the world and once *in* the world. But (S2) cannot exist next to the world, because there is nothing that is next to the world! The same applies to (S3) and every other field of sense. Thus, it is impossible for the world to appear in a field of sense that appears next to other fields of sense. That is to say, from this it follows that the other fields of sense cannot exist at all. We can also express this a bit more casually: *the world is not found in the world.*

Beyond all of this there is another problem. If the world appears in (S1), in which the world appears, it differs from the world which appears in (S1). The world that appears is not identical to the world in which it

appears. That the world is not found in the world is easy
to understand independently of this somewhat formal
line of argumentation. Let us take the field of vision,
for example. In this domain one never sees the visual
field itself but only the visible objects: the neighbors, the

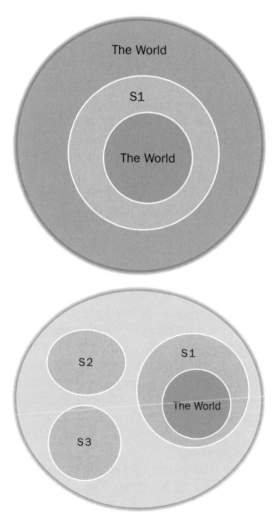

Figures 1 and 2

coffee house, the moon, or the sunset. At best one could attempt to represent the visual field pictorially: if I had the talent, say, to draw the visual field that is right in front of me, I would be able to see a picture of my visual field. But obviously this picture would not be my visual field but only another thing in my visual field. The same applies to the world: whenever we consider ourselves to have understood the world, we have only a copy or a picture of the world before us. We cannot grasp the world conceptually because there is no field of sense to which it belongs. The world does not appear on the stage of the world; it does not step up and introduce itself to us.

In *Escape from the Planet of the Apes*, the third part of the classic film series *Planet of the Apes*, Dr Otto Hasslein develops a certain theory of time which explains how it is possible for the apes to be brought back from the future into the past. Hasslein's theory is that one can understand time only if one interprets it as a kind of "infinite regress." He explains this to viewers of a news broadcast in which he appears – in the film these viewers are the apes of the future, and of course we are viewers of the film – with the help of an illuminating example. We see a landscape in a painting. We know that someone painted the landscape. So we can also imagine a painting in which a painting appears along with the painter who painted it. But this painting is also painted, and absolutely not by the same painter. For at best he paints the painting in the painting. Thus, we can once again imagine a painting in which we see the painter who paints a picture, in which a painter paints the original landscape, and so on, *ad infinitum* – an infinite regression.

The painter who paints everything cannot paint himself in the activity of painting. The painted painter is never completely identical with the painter who is painting. In this scene of the film it is worth noting that we, the viewers, find ourselves in the same condition as the apes from the future. We see the same television picture as they do. Interestingly, the television viewers in the background of the screen on the television see a mirror in which one observes the moderator and Dr Hasslein, whereby at least three perspectives symbolically coalesce: the apes from the future, the moderator and Dr Hasslein, and us. The film – our world – consists of an unending interweaving.

In an eerie and alarming way many films lead us to this truth. The very stage setting in Vincenzo Natali's film *Cube* is especially terrifying. In *Cube*, different people initially find themselves isolated from one another in a cube-shaped room. Each of these rooms has different doors which in each case lead to another cube-shaped room. Some of the rooms are set with life-threatening booby-traps. As the film proceeds it turns out that the number combinations which are found between the rooms form a cycle of movement, the knowledge of which leads out of the cube. Outside of the cube there is only an emptiness, a nothingness that at the end of the film appears as bright light.

The film gives up on the representation of an external world in a forceful way and for this reason can serve as an illustration of a significant fact: there are an infinite number of fields of sense which are interwoven in infinitely many ways, some of which are also absolutely isolated from other fields of sense. This unending interweaving takes place, however, in the middle of nothing, thus nowhere specific at all. Each particular location can only be determined from within a field of sense; there is no beyond.

In his own original, satirical way, the German novelist and poet Jean Paul portrays this condition in his *Biography of a Wit* of 1785: "he always aspired to write books . . . he wanted to write one in which he wanted to prove that beings did indeed have existence, but existence itself did not."[25]

The world does not exist. If the world were to exist, it would have to appear in a field of sense, but that is impossible. However, this insight is not merely destructive, for it does not just tell us that the existence of the world is not to be expected. It can also be made fruitful if we want to understand what exists.

The Super-Thought

Let us call the thesis that the world does not exist the MAIN PRINCIPLE OF NEGATIVE ONTOLOGY. Against this stands the FIRST MAIN PRINCIPLE OF POSITIVE ONTOLOGY, which claims that, necessarily, there exist an infinite number of fields of sense. We can clarify the first main principle of positive ontology with a thought experiment. Let us imagine that there is only one individual object, let us say a blue cube. Nevertheless, if this and nothing else were the only object that existed, there would be no field of sense in which the blue cube might appear. The cube would also cease to exist, because a thing only exists if the fields of sense in which it appears also exist. If there were only one single object, there would be no objects at all, for the purportedly completely single object must appear in a field of sense in order to exist. A single thing is nothing, or, as Aimee Mann sings in the soundtrack to Thomas Anderson's film *Magnolia*, "one is the loneliest number."

Consequently there is at the very least one object and one field of sense. Now, at least one further field of sense must exist. For in order for there to be a single field of sense, according to the main principle of negative ontology, there must be another one in which the first field of sense appears. Thus there is at least one object and two fields of sense.

But we have already seen that, by "object," one

should merely understand what we are able to think about by means of truth-apt thoughts. Things in the narrow sense are a kind of object but also themselves fields of sense. Therefore the originally single object and the two fields of sense, which must be taken for granted, are actually three objects of our thinking. From this it follows that they exist at least in the field of sense of our thinking, so that, once more, we have taken up another field of sense.

In this connection we can propose another thesis, the SECOND MAIN PRINCIPLE OF POSITIVE ONTOLOGY: every field of sense is an object. From this it immediately follows that, for every field of sense, there is a field of sense in which it appears. The world is the sole exception, as it cannot be a field of sense, for it cannot appear, on account of which it cannot be an object.

Still, have we not now irrevocably ensnared ourselves in a contradiction? Have we not thought about the world? If we have thought about the world, then it surely exists, namely as an object that appears in our thoughts. Because the objects of our thought exist in our thoughts, there is a field of sense (our thoughts) in which the world appears. Thus, the world must nevertheless exist, mustn't it?

If the world existed in our thoughts, our thoughts could not exist in the world. Otherwise there would be a second world, which would consist of our thoughts and "the world" (in the sense of the object of our thought). Thus, we would not have succeeded in picking out the real world, after all. Just as the brilliant American television series *Seinfeld* (well, the similarity of the name to "fields of sense" is no accident) has taught us, our life is a "show about nothing." Everything that exists, everything that appears, in the end shows us that the world does not exist. For everything exists only because the world does not exist. One cannot think about the world.

What one understands when one attempts to think about it is nothing – more exactly, it is actually "less than nothing." Every thought about the world would have to be at least a thought in the world. We cannot think the world from above or from the outside, and for this reason we literally cannot think about the world. Thoughts about the world "as a whole" are not capable of being true; they do not have any object to which they refer so that they might turn out to be either true or false. Thoughts about the world are radically empty thoughts.

I hope that you will still allow me another turn of the screw of reflection. For now I should like to pursue a slightly acrobatic idea. This acrobatic idea consists in our reflecting on a thought which at the same time thinks about the whole world and about itself. This thought might be able to save the world and bring it back into existence. Let us call it the "super-thought." The SUPER-THOUGHT is the thought that thinks about the whole world and about itself at the same time. The super-thought thinks itself and everything else all at once.

The greatest metaphysician of all time, Georg Wilhelm Friedrich Hegel, introduced and justified this (unfortunately false) idea on the basis of some ancient Greek ideas in his *Science of Logic*, one of the best (and most difficult) books of philosophy of all time. Hegel's name for the super-thought is "the absolute idea," and one can easily see that this name for the phenomenon was completely adequate. The super-thought is the best idea, so to speak, which one can realize, precisely the absolute idea. Accordingly, we can now give the claim that there is a super-thought a name: ABSOLUTE IDEALISM is the thesis that a super-thought exists.

The only problem is that absolute idealism is arguably false. If the super-thought were true, it would need to exist. But in which field of sense does it appear? If it appeared in itself, the problem of the world returns: the super-thought cannot appear in itself, because then the

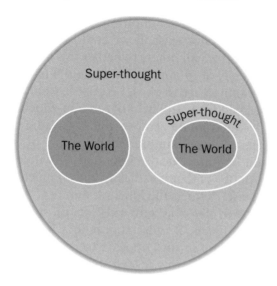

Figure 3

world would appear in itself as just another object in the world. This thought is illustrated in figure 3.

Of course, under greater scrutiny this figure is again seen to be incomplete and inadequate. For in the super-thought, which is found in the super-thought, the super-thought is found once again – an infinite interweaving. In this light it should be quite evident that the all-encompassing thing cannot appear in itself. The all-encompassing super-thought is inaccessible to us not only because we lack the sufficient time to think it through, but also because there is no field of sense in which it can appear. It does not exist.

Nihilism and Non-Existence

Let us return to an earthly and intuitive level, so to speak, and again imagine a blue cube. If it were to stand all by itself and were completely isolated from other objects, it could not exist. If we could isolate one individual object from all others (whether this be in thought, in the universe, or in any object domain whatsoever), it would instantly cease to exist, because it would be completely isolated from any field of sense in which it might appear. If we were to remove the blue cube from all fields of sense it would implode in a manner of speaking and would be ontologically impotent. It would simply be gone. An object that is radically and completely alone does not exist. "One is the loneliest number."

In order for any object to exist at all, it cannot be completely isolated. It must appear in a field of sense. This field of sense in turn appears to be too isolated to be able to exist. For this reason this field of sense also appears in a further field of sense, and so on. We never come to an end; in this way we never achieve the last field of sense in which everything appears – the world. Rather, the world is always deferred, on account of which all fields of sense that we can imagine (at least in our thoughts) exist except for the world itself. We cannot conceive the world at all, because the world that is conceived cannot be identical with the world in which we think about the world.

One can imagine the unending deferral of the world as a form of FRACTAL ONTOLOGY. Fractals are geometrical structures that consist of an infinite number of copies of themselves. Famous examples are the Pythagoras tree (see figure 4) and the Sierpinski triangle (see figure 5).

The non-existent world is copied within itself an infinite number of times, so to speak; there are many worlds, which are in turn composed of many worlds.

For this reason we only ever know sections of the infinite. An overview of the whole is impossible, because the whole does not exist at all. In the beautiful words of Rilke:

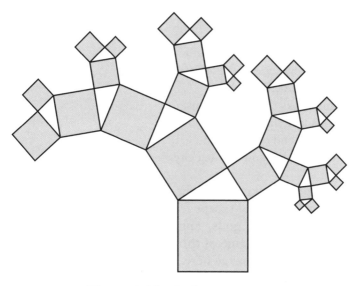

Figure 4 The Pythagoras tree

Figure 5 The Sierpinski triangle

We behold creation's face as though
reflected in a mirror
misted out with our breath.
Sometimes a speechless beast
lifts its docile head
and looks right through us.
This is destiny: to be opposites,
always and only to face
one another and nothing else.[26]

Admittedly Rilke was of the opinion that there is still a
way out, a kind of escape from infinity, which he attrib-
utes to animals, gods, angels, children, and even the
dead – a poetic game of thought, with which we luckily
do not have to engage here.

Are we not completely lost? If the world does not
exist, and instead there are just an infinite number of
fields of sense, doesn't everything finally break down?
Will everything now be completely indeterminate and
chaotic? How do we know exactly which level we
occupy? Is everything that we perceive arranged as a
kind of elementary particle in a great field of sense, in
which a much larger person thinks the same thoughts?

After all, in geometry one can distinguish the levels
on which one finds oneself through formal operations.
However, how does one mark the levels of reality on
which we live? Or, in our case, how do we actually
know which fields of sense we occupy? If in the end an
infinite explosion of senses takes place in the middle of
nothing, how can we locate ourselves? Doesn't everything sink into nothingness?

This worry is closely connected to the so-called phenomenon of nihilism. MODERN NIHILISM (from
Latin "nihil" = "nothing"), which occurs in many different guises, claims that everything is without meaning
or that everything comes down to nothing. We struggle and toil on our small unimportant planet, which

moves in an infinite expanse without our being able to explain where we find ourselves or what all of it actually means. According to Einstein's theory of relativity, it is not even easy to state at what time we exist because there is no single, absolute simultaneity; there is no simple now in which all events, which are occurring right "now," can be measured. Some physicists and metaphysicians even think that time itself does not exist, that actually everything has already happened and that time is only a kind of illusion of "moving" beings.[27] Do we still live a meaningful life, or does the infinite interweaving of fields of sense destroy all meaning, all importance?

Not in the least, rather the opposite: in the face of so much meaning, we could lose orientation in the world. Perhaps this is what the famous Greek proto-philosopher Thales of Miletus meant when according to tradition, he said: "Everything is full of gods." The German philosopher Hans Blumenberg saw a problem with this and spelled it out in a series of fine and provocative books.[28] In his view, Thales wanted to simplify the overwhelming infinity of gods and accordingly invented a modern scientific idea – the idea that, in the final analysis, everything that exists consists of a single substance: "Everything is water" (as an inhabitant of a seaport, water was somewhat important to him). Indeed, while today we know that everything is not water, we still think that there exists a single world substance out of which everything is made – matter/energy, strings, or whatever turns out to be the right way of looking at this.

However, Thales' principle is false in two ways. It is certainly false that everything is water (some stuff is fire and some is earth). But it is also false that there is something or other that is everything. "Everything" means nothing. The expression "everything" does not refer to anything determinate. As a matter of fact, one can meaningfully say: "All lions prefer gazelles" or "All rivers contain water," but one cannot say: "Everything is X." For otherwise the absolutely universal X – a most universal concept under which everything would fall – would exist. This absolutely universal concept would once again be the world, which we already know does not exist. For this reason there is no theory which describes everything, because something like "absolutely everything" cannot exist.

But doesn't the fractal ontology which I am suggesting claim, for example, that everything is identical, that all things are small copies of the world, which only exist in connection with one another and are thereby differentiated from the world? Then it would have committed the same error as Thales and claimed that "Everything consists of fields of sense" or that "Fields of sense are all that exists."

Let us imagine this in a more visual way: if in each case fields of sense exist only in other fields of sense, because one can never isolate any field of sense, is "reality" a kind of infinite being interweaving in itself – an infinitely compound eye? Do we find ourselves in one of the segments of the infinite eye without being able to determine in which one we exist, because no segment is differentiated from any other? Such a situation would be, so to speak, "enough to drive you crazy."

However, I can put your mind at ease. We do not find ourselves in this condition, or, more exactly, my arguments do not suggest that we find ourselves in this or a similar condition. For only if the fields of sense were not differentiated from one another at all would there be a smooth surface of fields of sense – an infinitely interweaving being, an infinitely large compound eye. Fields of sense are quite diverse: a boat ride on the Amazon is fundamentally different from a dream or a physical equation. Citizenship is something completely different from medieval painting. Even though fields of sense sometimes overlap, there is no overall ground on which they stand, no overall structure (such as that of the infinite eye).

What makes a field of sense a field of sense is not exhausted by its being a field of sense. It is precisely for this reason that I speak about fields of sense and not about object domains. The difference is the following: a domain has the tendency to be neutral regarding the question concerning what is found in it. Let us take a house somewhere in Brooklyn. The only thing I know about this house, say, is that it has seven rooms. These rooms are object domains. Nothing about the rooms as such needs to change if we put some furniture there. No matter what one finds in them, they remain rooms. Even an empty room is still a room. In contrast, fields of sense are not to be understood without the orientation and arrangement of the objects which appear in them. This is similar to magnetic fields: one sees magnetic fields only when one disperses certain objects over them which thereby show their form. Fields of sense are determined through objects that appear in them. Objects are closely bound up with the sense of fields of sense.

In this way one can recognize that identity or individuality is essential for our understanding of fields of sense. In order for several fields of sense to be able to exist at all, they must be differentiated from one another. What differentiates fields of sense from one another is their meaning, which we must recognize if we want to know in which field of sense we find ourselves. The ontological concept of the field of sense tells us only that there must be many fields of sense and that they differ from one another. It does not tell us anything concrete or more substantial, such as what fields of sense there are and how they are constituted. For this we need other sciences or forms of knowing besides ontology: experience, our senses, language, thought – in short: the reality of human knowledge. Ontology shows us only that reality cannot ultimately consist of undifferentiated fields of sense, which are everywhere structurally identical. But which fields of sense there are, the list of concrete fields of sense, is an achievement not of ontology but of the empirical sciences.

This is also why we are fallible when it comes to figuring out to which field of sense an object belongs and on what grounds. For we might inadvertently locate ourselves in the wrong field of sense. In this sense one would be mistaken, for example, if one thought that there are trolls in Norway. For trolls may indeed exist in Nordic mythology (which in turn exists in Norway), but there have never been trolls in Norway outside of mythology. For what belongs to the field of sense "Norway" is found within its national borders or concerns citizenship of the country. Trolls are neither found in the area which we call "Norway," nor are they Norwegian citizens. Thus, no trolls exist in Norway, even though they do exist in Nordic mythology.

Against this background we can solve a great riddle of the history of philosophy. This riddle arises from the question regarding how negative statements about existence (so-called negative existentials) are to be understood. Negative existentials are statements which claim that something does not exist. These statements have caused philosophers headaches for millennia. The reason for this lies in the fact that we apparently assume that something exists when we attribute a property to it. If I say that Judith has a headache, I assume both that Judith exists and that she has a headache. Otherwise Judith could not have a headache. If this applies to all statements, then this also applies to all negative statements of existence. If we claim that Judith does not own a car, then we insinuate the existence of both Judith and cars, with the caveat that at the present time Judith does not own a car. But what is the case when we claim that Judith does not exist? Do we then presume that Judith and existing objects exist only to ensure that Judith does not belong to the class of existing objects? If Judith has the property of non-existence, must Judith not exist? In the end something that does not exist cannot have any properties. But apparently Judith has the property of not existing: thus she must exist. This amounts to the contradiction that Judith must exist if she doesn't exist.

Often this problem is also associated with the idea that we cannot say anything about nothingness. When we say something about nothingness, we seem to assume that it exists, as well as that it is something determinate, namely nothingness. In this way we would have fallen short of nothingness, for neither is it something determinate, nor does it exist. At best, nothingness appears to be that thing which we "grasp" whenever we do not think, which means of course that we cannot grasp it in thought.

These problems turn out to be pseudo-problems. Ultimately, we must understand negative existentials as well as nothingness in a completely different way.

What are we claiming when we say that something doesn't exist? When we claim, for instance, that witches do not exist, what do we actually mean? Let's take a closer look and formulate a true negative existential:

Witches do not exist.

Against this someone could very well object that witches do exist – for instance, in Goethe's *Faust*, in *The Blair Witch Project*, in the confused heads of Spanish inquisitors, and during Carnival in Cologne. Thus, the proposition

Witches exist

is equally true. But now we wind up with an unpleasant contradiction:

Witches exist and witches do not exist.

Admittedly one should see right away that there is no real contradiction here. For we have not said that witches exist *simpliciter* and that witches do not exist *simpliciter*. It is in each case a question of context: when we deny that something exists, we are always denying that it appears in a specific field of sense. And, without risking a contradiction, we can claim in the same breath that it appears in another field of sense. There are witches, though not in the sense intended by the Spanish inquisitors. If I say that there is not a McDonald's in my part of the city, surely I have not claimed that no McDonald's exist at all. This applies universally: statements about existence, whether they are positive or negative, always refer only to one field of sense or to several fields of sense, but never to all and least of all to one all-encompassing field of sense. Exactly because there is no all-encompassing field of sense, it follows that existence is always relative, namely relative to one or more fields of sense.

Here some readers might want to raise an objection: Does existence not contrast with hallucination, error, fiction, and mere imagination? If we say that moles exist, are we not saying that moles are not merely imagined, that they *really* exist? Or, if it is about aliens, surely we do not want to know whether aliens exist in our imagination but, rather, whether they *really* exist somewhere out there.

This objection differentiates falsely between *existence* and *imagination*. For figments of the imagination also exist, and much exists only in the imagination. Additional provisos such as "exists *only in*" and "*really* exists" do not undermine the relativity. For example, one can see this in a discussion between two interpreters of *Faust*. The one claims that there are no witches in *Faust*, that Faust only hallucinates them. The other objects that there really are witches in *Faust*, that Faust is not imagining them, for they are real in the world of the drama. The difference between "really" and "merely imagined" concerns fields of sense just as much as the worlds of drama, which are "merely imagined." In what is "merely imagined" the contrast between "what is real" and "what is merely imagined," which is called "embedded fiction," also applies.

For this reason existence is not primarily connected with the idea that something is found in the universe or that something is a physical, material object. Otherwise one could not discuss the question concerning which fictional characters really exist within a novel and which do not. Existence is always existence in a specific field of sense. The question is always what field of sense it concerns, and we are often mistaken about this. Institutions that persecute witches have confused figments of their imagination with women living in Europe. However, no woman who has ever lived in Europe or anywhere else was a witch in the officially intended sense of witch hunters. Accordingly witches always exist only in the minds of their persecutors and have never existed on earth. No witches appear in the field of sense "earth," but they certainly do in the field of sense "representations of early modern witch hunters." It is thus a completely legitimate claim that in a few early modern representations there were witches or that there are witches in *Faust*.

The External and the Internal World

Unfortunately many philosophers are lagging behind the progress that modern philosophy has made since Kant. They continue to think, like some materialist philosophers of early modernity, that there is a so-called external world which affects our sense organs and triggers representations of itself within our minds. While the external world simply exists, our representations can be true or false; the external world is neither true nor false, but simply there. But it is simply false that there is an external world, on the one hand, and next to it our representations of it triggered by the external world. For this assumes a false ontological worldview, namely a picture of the world as a whole insofar as it claims that there are things – mind and world – and that they are related by the mind having representations of the external world triggered by its denizens.

The background mistake leading to this consists in bringing science into connection with a worldview. This is – by the way – no philosophical wisdom. It is already well known to me and many other adults of my generation through the *Muppet Show*, whose characters – like those in so many children's books and, indeed, like many children – are so much wiser than the followers of a purported "scientific worldview." In the *Muppet Show* there is a recurring sketch called "Pigs in Space." The title says everything already. For above all it is about educating children that we are not simply pigs in space. We are not simply eating, digesting, and calculating animals lost in an infinitely stupid expanse of meaningless galaxies, but human beings, and that means, above all, beings who know that they exist and find themselves in complicated relationships. In one version of "Pigs in Space" the spaceship "Pig Filth" reels hopelessly lost in space. In the first scene we see how the captain attempts to draw a map of the infinite expanse: the sideways figure 8 representing infinity, however, ends up looking like a duckling. In the meantime Miss Piggy cries out in terror: "Oh no, no, no. We are lost in this endless expanse of space. Why don't we just admit it!" She suddenly suffers an existential crisis. In response the captain just says: "Once before I was in a similarly desperate situation and nonetheless found my way out." Suddenly the pigs realize that they are crossing a "field with deadly snack-waves," which causes the captain's pencil to taste like prunes. The waves "transform everything on board into something edible." The pigs move into a field of sense in which everything is edible; their spaceship turns into a place in which only eating matters.

In fact, the so-called scientific worldview assumes that people are rather like pigs in space. It confuses existence with the domain of what is accessible via the senses and projects the human need for meaning onto the vastness of the galaxies. No wonder that everything appears without meaning and empty of sense if one sees people as pigs in space (even though, admittedly, we sometimes act like pigs in space)!

If we are concerned with pictures of the world, reality as a whole, or actuality, we normally move quite a distance from our everyday experiences. For this reason we all too easily overlook what Heidegger designated as "the leap."[29] We gaze, as it were, at reality from outside and ask how it exists. From this remarkable distance it appears to many as though the world were out there, as though we were sitting in a kind of room or movie theatre watching a reality to which we do not really belong. From this fantasy arises the concept of the "external world." But obviously we are in the thick of it, although very often we have no idea where we are inside this reality, what it all means, or what film we have landed in.

However, insofar as we are so far removed from our actual life, we have already made many theoretical decisions that have gone unnoticed. Actually it must be said that mostly we do not make these decisions consciously; rather, they have already been decided for us, because world pictures are bandied about in the media, through systems of education, and through institutions of all kinds. We are constantly being bombarded with manipulated photos of the Hubble Telescope (for they are unacceptably edited, and attractively colored) and models of the newest elementary particles, which are designed to create the impression that we are receiving definitive insight into the universe and the fundamental nature of reality. While earlier preachers of all kinds disseminated their message in Latin or other holy languages, today scientists and experts are consulted who tell us that in principle there are only elementary particles (or what have you), and that we people are actually only pigs in space who are fundamentally interested in reproducing and eating. The holy language of the day consists of mathematical equations, diagrams, and deep field shots of the universe designed to impress the laymen and suggest metaphysical expertise. All of this has become credible because we are told that the way in which we experience life is an illusion – an age-old religious slogan. The world should be that thing which one sees whenever one takes up "the view from nowhere," as the American philosopher Thomas Nagel has termed it.[30] Mind you, Nagel has shown that we cannot attain the view from nowhere, that it merely represents a confused ideal after which we strive in order to remove our own personal interests as much as possible when it comes to the question of truth.

Do you remember how the world appeared to you as an eight-year-old? Remember your hopes, wishes, and fears, and how you imagined your life to be in ten or more years! Remember your old friends, family parties, vacations, the first day of summer, an important insight in school! Now make clear to yourself how much your perception has changed as the time has passed. What you are thereby observing is a change of fields of sense, the transition from one field of sense to another. To see this we do not have to bother ourselves with our whole life story. We are always experiencing changes in fields of sense, however unimportant the moment.

I am currently writing these lines on my veranda; it is the first summery day at the end of April 2012. While writing these lines, every once in a while I look at a beautiful church tower that I can see from my veranda. My neighbor's child yells something at me. Little David plays with a garden hose and tries to get my attention. A glider passes right by, and I think about a conversation with Thomas Nagel about the ideas which I am just now writing down. In so doing I imagine myself in his office at Washington Square Park in New York. He sits behind his desk and has a very thoughtful and friendly way about him. Now I come out of my reverie and feel a trace of thirst. I sip on my tea, which is sitting next to me.

What has taken place here is one of the small trips through fields of sense which we take a hundred times a day. We wander from memories to bodily impressions, such as the pleasant warmth or uncomfortable pants, all the way to theoretical thoughts or noises. We ask ourselves how we are supposed to get along with our fellow human beings (for example, with little David) or how the next sentence should unfold. We move unremittingly through uncountable fields of sense and certainly never arrive at an ultimate field of sense that encompasses everything. Even when I paint the infinite vastness of galaxies or engage in thought experiments, I am still only wandering through other fields of sense. It is as though we are sent from field of sense to field of sense. Even when we consciously take our life into our own hands and act in a goal-oriented way, we are met with uncountable contingencies at every moment: smells which we have not expected, people whom we do not know, situations to which we have never been exposed. Our life is a single movement through various fields of sense, and in each case we produce or stumble upon the connections. By typing these lines, for instance, I take into account the field of sense "first summery day on which I write these lines" and place the appearing objects in it. For this reason there is a church tower and little David in these pages – everyday details, though nonetheless important.

Admittedly, our ordinary language is hardly sufficient to lead us to that which we experience, on account of which poets such as Rainer Maria Rilke have in the end proved themselves to be the better phenomenologists, the saviors of appearances. In one of his *New Poems* he describes childhood in exactly the way in which I think about the ontology of fields of sense:

> It would be good to give much thought, before
> you try to find words for something so lost,
> for those long childhood afternoons you knew
> that vanished so completely – and why?
>
> We're still reminded: sometimes by a rain,
> but we can no longer say what it means;
> life was never again so filled with meeting,
> with reunion and with passing on
>
> as back then, when nothing happened to us
> except what happens to things and creatures:
> we lived their world as something human,
> and became filled to the brim with figures.
>
> And became as lonely as a shepherd
> and as overburdened by vast distances,
> and summoned and stirred as from far away,
> and slowly, like a long new thread,
> introduced into that picture-sequence
> where now having to go on bewilders us.[31]

We humans rightly want to know what it all means and whether we fit into the larger scheme of things. One should not underestimate this metaphysical drive, for it makes us what we are. The human being is a meta-physical animal, an animal for whom it is a concern to determine its "place in the cosmos," as Max Scheler put it in a classic little book.[32] However, we must be very cautious with our answer to the question concerning the meaning of it all. For we cannot simply skip over our experience and act as if there existed a tremendous world in which our experience actually has no place. In his book *Risky Proximity to Life*, the philosopher Wolfram Hogrebe aptly described this modern fantasy of the cosmos as "cold home."[33]

The world in which we live shows itself as a single continuous transition from field of sense to field of sense, as a coalescence and interweaving of them. It does not reveal an altogether universal cold home, because such a thing does not exist.

It is indisputable that we see the world "from the standpoint of a human being,"[34] as Kant said. Still, this does not mean that we cannot know what it is in itself. We know how the world is in itself from the standpoint of the human being.

In the next chapter we will see that none of this is directed against actual scientific results or the acquisition of knowledge about the nature of the universe. I do not even have an intention to undercut their objectivity or their capacity to grasp things as they are in themselves. We must simply avoid confusing the objectivity of the sciences with the exploration of the world. The natural sciences investigate their domain of objects and are very often right and sometimes wrong, which is why they have a history that is hopefully governed by a rational process of trial and error. That we overlook our own everyday experience while we prematurely create world pictures and in the process forget ourselves is not just a natural fact about us, but a bad habit, a laziness of thought, which luckily we can overcome.

In contrast to the modern worldview which tries to reduce the importance of actual self-knowledge by focusing on the integration of our organisms in the zoo of our planet, philosophy in the ancient Greek tradition, as well as the ancient Indian and Chinese traditions, was largely focused on the question of who we are. Philosophy arises from the desire for self-knowledge and not from the desire to erase ourselves from the world formula. The insight that the world does not exist, that there exist only fields of sense which proliferate in infinite variations, allows us to return to an acceptance of the fact that we are human beings and not zombies or neuromachines, and it asserts this minimal humanism independently of any specific worldview. All worldviews are false, because they assume that there is a world about which we can have a view. As we will see, we can dispense with the world without giving up on science. In fact, we must defend ourselves against the unreasonable demand of having to explain everything, an unreasonable demand which nothing and no one can fulfill.

IV

The Worldview of Natural Science

We live in modernity, and modernity is the age of science and enlightenment. Above all, "Enlightenment" signifies an event in the eighteenth century, which many see as a pinnacle of modernity, though others, such as Theodor Adorno and Max Horkheimer in their joint book *Dialectic of Enlightenment*, see it as a clear precursor of the political disasters of the twentieth century.[35] With this book Adorno and Horkheimer became the founders of Critical Theory, which is critical by virtue of its goal of unmasking the warped ideological assumptions of their own time. In a subtle way, a similar critique of the Enlightenment was also worked out in the French philosophy of the twentieth century, for example in the work of the philosopher, sociologist, and historian Michel Foucault.

However, one should not identify modernity as the age of science with the historical process of the Enlightenment, for modernity had already begun in the early modern era, starting in the fifteenth century with the scientific revolution – which admittedly also resulted in political revolutions – while the Enlightenment commenced in the eighteenth century. The scientific revolution essentially consisted in the process whereby the entire ancient and medieval worldview came apart at the seams. The world turned out to be ordered not in the least in the way it had been conceived in Europe for thousands of years, since the beginnings of early Greek philosophy. The ancient idea of a cosmos came under pressure, even though it was almost immediately replaced by just another cosmos, another order, whose outlines were described by modern natural science. But, in this new order, there was no special place for man, which was perfectly in line with the discovery that man misconstrued the cosmos for so long. Mistrust in the human faculties underlying our earlier apparent knowledge followed on the heels of these early (from our contemporary perspective, naïve) insights into space and the mechanics of heavenly bodies. Modernity begins with the decentralization of humanity and its life environment, the planet earth. Humanity grasped that it was located in a much larger context than it had previously dared to dream, and that this context was in no way tailored to human needs. Yet, from this, a scientific worldview was prematurely inferred in which humans are no longer to be found. The human being began to erase itself from the world and to turn the world into its cold home: it began to identify the world with the universe. In so doing the human being had underhandedly smuggled itself into the worldview. For the assumption that the world is essentially a world without spectators cannot be posited without the spectator, which one wants to do away with. Insofar as this is still a worldview, we can expect that it is driven and maintained by some desire on the part of the spectator. This does not make it false, but it does make it inadequate to the extent to which the spectator loses sight of himself. And this is exactly what happened and what drives the current fantasy of a post- or transhuman age. Humanity chases after the dream of overcoming itself so as to make it true that there really is only a meaningless universe by eliminating meaning, or what we take to be meaning.

Besides this, it is especially interesting that the idea of a cold home without spectators arose just as the then inhabitants of Europe came upon other people with a genuinely different home. The discovery of the Americas is the really striking discovery that more exists than had previously been assumed. It was rather irritating for the Europeans at that time that the others should be recognized as fully valid human beings who differed from the Europeans. As a result of this encounter, the place of humanity in the cosmos was put into question. As the remarkable and brilliant Brazilian anthropologist Eduardo Viveiros de Castro emphasized, the gradual expulsion of the supposed "wild things" became a motor for the assumption that the universe could do without people completely. As he also showed, many of the indigenous communities which are still found within the frontiers of Brazil today have progressed onto-logically much further than the scientific worldview, for they do not assume that there is really only a world without spectators but, rather, they have grappled with the question "Why are there spectators?" and what this actually means. Viveiros de Castro therefore sees these communities through the eyes of an anthropologist, from whom we can learn that we cannot get around the question concerning who we are as human beings.[36] He calls this "symmetrical anthropology," which, in the final analysis, means that both the European discoverers and the indigenous communities are people who study one another, such that the different ways in which they make sense of one another are on an equal footing. The European discoverers simply were not superior in their understanding of what it is to be a human being, as they even had problems recognizing indigenous people as human beings! This failure lies at the heart of modern racism, and it ushered in one of the biggest genocides of modernity.

Independently   of   the   difficult   historical   and philosophical question as to whether modernity led to the Enlightenment, and the Enlightenment in turn to the great political catastrophes of the last century, as strict followers of Adorno and Horkheimer would have to assume, it can be stated plainly and without bias that it is of the greatest advantage to live in an epoch of science. It is simply better to go to a dentist with contemporary knowledge and modern technology than to go to Plato's dentist. Even traveling has become significantly more comfortable. When an ancient Greek philosopher from Athens was invited to a lecture in Sicily, he had to make his journey on a very uncomfortable ship that was powered by rowing slaves. (And certainly the dinner after the lecture would not have been very desirable by modern-day standards, since at that time there were not even tomatoes in Europe – these first arrived on the continent following the voyages of discovery in early modernity. Moreover, the ancient Greeks did not have a great abundance of spices. No wonder that the struggle for the sea route to the spice paradise of India was an important factor in the development of modernity. Spices originally drove the development of the scientific worldview, a fact mythologically coded in Frank Herbert's science-fiction masterpiece *Dune*.)

Despite all of their great scientific achievements, the ancient Greeks believed that the universe was quite limited – no doubt they would have been surprised to find out how many solar systems, according to current estimations and calculations, exist in the Milky Way. What is more, in Greek philosophy the human being was at the center of all events, which is also an overstatement. The thesis that the human being is the "measure of all things," attributed to the philosopher Protagoras, has gone down in history as the HOMO MENSURA PRINCIPLE. Against this, modernity posits the SCIENTIA MENSURA PRINCIPLE, as elucidated by the American philosopher Wilfrid Sellars.

But, speaking as a philosopher, I am quite prepared to say that the common sense world of physical objects in Space and Time is unreal – that is, that there are no such things. Or, to put it less paradoxically, that in the dimension of describing and explaining the world, science is the measure of all things, of what is that it is, and of what is not that it is not.[37]

In the age of science, the world of the human being is looked upon with suspicion as the domain of illusion, while the world of science, the universe, is advanced as the measure of objectivity. The question is no longer how the world appears to us, but how it is in itself.

However, given the previous chapters, we should be prepared to call this general background of the scientific worldview into question. From fields of sense ontology it follows that there cannot be a fundamental level to reality – the world in itself – that only ever presents itself in distorted ways to our registries. SCIENTISM, the belief that only the natural sciences understand the fundamental level of reality, namely the world in itself, while all other knowledge claims are always reducible to the sciences or, at any rate, should be measured by these, is simply false.

Neither a critique of any one specific discipline nor a critique of the ideal of modern science in our investigation of the universe follows from this. Scientific progress yields medical, gastronomic, economic, and even political progress. The more scientific knowledge we acquire, the closer we come to overcoming old errors based on false assumptions about the workings of the universe. There is no doubt about that. Aside from the question regarding how the Enlightenment and science relate to each other, we can rest assured that scientific progress is welcome. However, scientific progress is not identical to progress in the natural sciences. There is progress in sociology, the fine arts, and philosophy, as well as developments in progress which take place completely beyond the course of science, such as progress in skateboarding or haute cuisine. There are also significant regresses, some of them triggered indirectly by modernity's achievements, some of them simply due to human forgetfulness.

Scientific achievements are of great benefit. When we state that we live in an age of science, this is a joyful message – a kind of honorary title. For we connect science to the absence of prejudice, as well as with knowledge, which can be communicated to every human being independently of their social status. Science proceeds in a way that is reproducible and verifiable for every individual who appropriates its methods. In this sense it is a democratic project, because it takes for granted the equality of human beings in light of the value of truth and the establishment of truth – which does not mean, by the way, that there are not better and worse scientists. Nevertheless, science is fundamentally a collective good. Unfortunately, access to this common good is mediated by power struggles that often merely confirm the power structure of a given society. This is particularly evident in the academic system in the English-speaking world, because access to education there is built on a brutal capitalist economic model. This threatens to disconnect science from the democratic hope of equality for all in light of the scientific method.

However, the situation now becomes difficult when one connects the honorary title "science" or the predicate "scientific" with a worldview. And that is on account of two general reasons, each of which speaks against a scientific worldview and against the scientific nature of worldviews as such. These reasons are themselves scientific, for they are well justified and are reproducible and verifiable for everyone, which also means that one can rebut, reject, or even refute them – which, however, one must first do scientifically and in a way that is comprehensible to all. Philosophy is a science in this sense, as it is an undertaking capable of proof and justification, against which one can raise objections. In the last two hundred years, especially in the wake of Kant, the concept of the world in particular was revolutionized in philosophy. Here too philosophy makes progress, which has put it in a position to undermine worldviews as such.

The first reason for the failure of the scientific worldview lies simply in the fact that the world does not exist. One cannot create a picture of something that does not exist and cannot exist even in thought. One cannot even invent the world. The other reason, which will play a larger role in this chapter, is related: we cannot create a picture of the world because we cannot look at the world from the outside. As I have already mentioned in connection with an insightful phrase from Thomas Nagel, we cannot attain the "view from nowhere." We always peer at reality from some standpoint or other. We are always *somewhere* and never view reality from *nowhere*.

The first reason for the failure of the scientific worldview is *ontological*. It shows that the scientific worldview is based upon demonstrably false assumptions, such that what follows from these assumptions must at the very least be false or unjustified. The second reason is *epistemological*. It is connected with the idea that we cannot take up a view from nowhere. Please note that it does not follow from this that we do not know anything or that we are only able to design models of the world without ever forging ahead to the facts themselves. It would be erroneous to assume that our convictions or scientific models sit before our mental eyes like distorting glasses, so that we only ever know the human world, the world that is interpreted according to our interests, but never the world as it is in itself. This corresponds to the postmodern overreaction to the correct insight that there is something ideological about science. But it was not science as such that was ideological all the while, but the worldview associated with it. For even the human world belongs to the world in itself, or, in the language of fields of sense ontology: some fields of sense are accessible only to people, and they are just as "real" as fields of sense which contain facts that people will never encounter.

The alleged scientific worldview fails on account of scientifically demonstrable reasons. If we investigate it methodologically and without prejudice, it crumbles in our fingers. Before we apply the conceptual magnifying glass and investigate more closely the clockwork of reasons and objections against any worldview, it is important to understand what the "scientific worldview" is supposed to achieve. Only when we become aware of that will we understand what the debate between religion and science, between the one scientific worldview and the many religious worldviews, is really about. We shall concern ourselves with this in greater detail in the following chapter.

Naturalism

Disciples of the scientific worldview often argue in the following way: there is just one nature, a domain unified by laws of nature. Nature is the domain of objects of the natural sciences, the universe. Accordingly, nothing exists that is supernatural or goes beyond nature. For what is supernatural or beyond nature would necessarily violate natural laws. Because nothing can violate the laws of nature (according to their definition), only nature exists. In short, the position that only nature exists, that only the universe exists, is known as NATURALISM.[38] According to this, only that which can be ontologically traced back to the domain of the natural sciences can exist; everything else is mere illusion.

Hilary Putnam, a philosopher who, like very few

others, has for many decades been intensively engaged with naturalism and the great achievements of natural science in the twentieth century (above all theoretical physics, but also computer science and research into the foundations of mathematics), has identified a certain anxiety in naturalism. In his most recent book, *Philosophy in the Age of Science*, he indicates that naturalism would like to treat the universe without irrational assumptions.[39] Explanations which are not scientifically reproducible and are weak or completely arbitrary according to scientific standards count among such irrational assumptions.

An example: let us imagine that someone tells us that the earth came into existence two weeks ago on a Thursday. In this case, being quite puzzled, we would retort that this couldn't be the case. For instance, in order for the Alps to exist, lengthy geological processes would have had to take place, which could not have come about in two weeks. The same applies to our own origins, especially because we are able to remember the time before that Thursday. Now, if our informant went on to explain that it is completely normal for freshly created human beings to foster these convictions, for they are more or less inscribed in them during their creation, any further discussion would be senseless. We would probably come to the conclusion that this so-called explanation is utterly arbitrary.

Now, naturalists think that every traditional explanation of the world as a whole, or some phenomena which are found in it, that makes use of non-natural objects such as God, an immaterial soul, spirits, or destiny is a case that constructs arbitrary hypotheses. For the naturalist, the assumption that God exists is an utterly arbitrary hypothesis alongside many others. According to naturalism, anyone who claims that God prescribed the Ten Commandments or that Krishna was the personification of divinity makes the same claim (from a formal point of view) as someone who worships the flying spaghetti monster.[40] Naturalism condemns religion as a competing explanation of the world because it takes it to be an unscientific hypothesis. It is therefore believed to be a competitor to religion on exactly the same level, as it assumes that there is simply nothing more to explain than the universe.

So far, so good. Indeed, we do not want to give the arbitrary invention of hypotheses any precedence. For this reason naturalism and the scientific worldview are recommended as a remedy to a dangerous poison: human capriciousness. If wish were the father of thought, we would quite often, if not always, be wrong.

Descartes, one of the founding fathers of the scientific worldview, declared exactly in this way why we are fallible and have the tendency to make mistakes. For him, this tendency consists primarily in our will overrunning reason: wish is the father of thought. As scientists we want to know the truth and to free ourselves from illusions. It is not about how we represent reality, but about how it is. For this reason, in the philosophy of early modernity, a general suspicion arises against human capriciousness and the imagination. From now on it is important to distinguish between the real world and fiction: the real world, the universe, is that which has absolutely nothing to do with our imagination.

Naturalism throws the baby out with the bathwater. For it seems that at least two criteria are applied in order to differentiate what is natural from what is supernatural.

1   The supernatural is the object of arbitrary hypothesis construction – that is, pure fabrication.
2   The supernatural violates natural laws.

Nevertheless, on these grounds alone it is not possible to argue against religion, which is usually held by its staunch defenders to be the enemy of the scientific worldview. Of course, such people are usually both utterly misguided about religion and whom they are combating and completely misinformed about history, an ignorance essential for their own belief system. For instance, they usually do not acknowledge that the Belgian priest Georges Lemaître is one of the earliest proponents of the Big Bang and that the Catholic Church did not have any trouble recognizing this. They often invoke Giordano Bruno, the great Italian philosopher, as some kind of atheist hero but do not mention that he was a Dominican who never gave up the concept of God. In fact, Bruno argued simply on the basis of classical metaphysical considerations known to philosophers since antiquity that the universe had to be infinite. He thought that this was the more adequate way of looking at God.

Historical and philosophical ignorance is especially apparent in the neo-atheist movement, which is propagated by authors such as Richard Dawkins,[41] Daniel Dennett or Lawrence Krauss. Neo-atheism associates religion with a religious worldview that stands in competition with science. In fact, in the United States there is a circle of religious fundamentalists who are of the opinion that evolutionary theory and modern cosmology are false, because God created the universe and animals at a specific point in time a few thousand years before the birth of Christ. Dawkins is correct that CREATIONISM – the thesis that God's intervention in nature explains nature better than the natural sciences – is simply a pseudo-explanation. It is not a scientific hypothesis to be taken seriously but, rather, is an arbitrary fabrication of human imagination – and in addition not especially old: it first arose in the nineteenth century, above all in Anglo-American Protestantism. In Germany it fortunately plays no role at all. In scientific theology in the German-speaking world it has virtually no proponents, which has to do with the tight-knit relationship between theology and philosophy. Creationism is not a natural ingredient of religion but a form of superstition. One should not prematurely equate the phenomenon of religion with creationism, which the neo-atheists justifiably attack.

The first verse of the book of Genesis, right at the beginning of the Bible, reads: "In the beginning God created the heaven and the earth."[42] Both naturalists and creationists interpret this sentence as a scientific hypothesis, and both are wrong about this from the perspective of scientific theology or the actual history of interpretations of this text. Both misconstrue the passage by boiling it down to the idea that a very powerful supernatural person, "God," some time ago, "at the beginning," created "heaven and earth," thus our planet and everything that is located outside of its atmosphere. As a scientific hypothesis this is simply false and falsified by any acceptable standard, and in this respect neo-atheism is without question correct. It is just nonsense to assume that God created the world, in the same way as a car manufacturer produces a car. This had already been rejected by the earliest metaphysical interpreters of this passage, both Jewish and Christian, a tradition that continued through the Middle Ages and was entirely ignored by creationist and neo-atheist readers alike.

If one pushes naturalism too far on the basis of the superficial insight that no supernatural mind has created the universe, one easily loses sight of many phenomena – governments, for example. Are governments supernatural objects which violate the laws of nature? If the criterion of the natural consists in the capacity to be investigated by the natural sciences, then governments are just as supernatural as God or the soul. Hypotheses or even knowledge about governments is just not to be expected from the natural sciences.

Our everyday knowledge of the fact that the Federal Republic of Germany has a government, a constitution, a history, etc., need not be replaced or enhanced by some "physics" or "biology" of government or even by "neuro-political science." These theory-mutants are just monsters of the scientistic imagination. Is the hypothesis that governments exist unscientific – pure capriciousness – because their existence cannot be decided by the natural sciences? How about the claim that everything we can really know can be decided by the natural sciences? Can that claim be decided scientifically? What would that even mean?!

Monism

If naturalism and the scientific worldview demanded of us only that we investigate reality without bias and in a methodologically controlled way, then it would be somewhat empty. Most educated people who live in societies with real freedom of speech agree with this suggestion anyway. Militant naturalists and neo-atheists therefore take a significant step beyond this minimal commitment to rationality and advocate a worldview that is based on a form of monism. This form is MATERIALISTIC MONISM, which holds that the universe is the one and only existing domain of objects and which identifies this with the totality of material entities, whose structure and law-like behavior can adequately be explained only with the aid of the natural sciences. This monism is a substantial claim which needs to be substantiated. It cannot simply be passed off as a self-evident article of faith. Naturalism fundamentally aims at a unified explanation of totality. It intends to give an overview of everything, of the whole, of all that is actual, maybe even of all that is possible. What one supposedly sees thereby – the world as it is in itself, reality or actuality as a whole – is ideally identical with a gigantic space-time receptacle, in which elementary particles are determined by natural laws and influence one another. Anything else should not exist. Things might be more complicated, though, if some multiverse hypothesis or some version of string theory turns out to be true. Nevertheless, it is assumed from the outset that energy/matter is the essence of what there is.

However, if this is the scientific worldview, then it is quite absurd for numerous reasons. To a certain degree it is worse than Pumuckl.* For Pumuckl really exists (for example, in *Master Eder and his Pumuckl*), but viewed completely from the point of view of materialistic monism he fails to exist at all. Materialistic monism fails for the same reason that every monism fails, because it posits a super-object, the world, that, for reasons of principle, cannot exist. Hence, the scientific worldview is actually not dependent upon materialistic objects at all. It is not even dependent upon the existence of physical objects. The very idea of the scientific method, of bias-free rational investigation, is not limited to the natural sciences. It is also the defining feature of scientific theology, comparative literature (at its best), political science, and just plain ordinary everyday knowledge.

A relatively simple argument against materialistic monism stems from the work of the American logician and philosopher Saul A. Kripke in his influential book *Naming and Necessity*.[43] It draws on a very simple observation. A proper name such as "Margaret Thatcher" designates a person. If I say that Margaret Thatcher was once the prime minister of the United Kingdom, I am referring to Margaret Thatcher, the former prime minister of the United Kingdom. Following Kripke, let us say

---

* Pumuckl is a supernatural mythological figure who is the main character in a German TV series for children.

that the person from then on called Margaret Thatcher
was given this name at baptism. At the moment of
"initial baptism" (to use Kripke's technical term) a
proper name is linked with a specific person. Now, if
someone were to ask me whether Margaret Thatcher
was still living, I would say that she died in 2013.

However, what is the case if there is another person
who is still alive and is also called Margaret Thatcher?
Does this mean that my claim that Margaret Thatcher
died in 2013 is false? Not at all, for I am talking
about the Margaret Thatcher who was the former
prime minister of the United Kingdom. Kripke assumes
that, from the moment of their initial baptism, the
person is "rigidly designated." This means that they are
uniquely picked out among all other persons by their
proper name, because there is a historical link (baptism) between that actual person and the name. Kripke
expresses this a bit more technically with his claim that
"rigid designators" refer to the same object in all possible worlds. This means that I can ask what Margaret
Thatcher would do, for example, in light of the current economic situation, despite the fact that she is not
alive to experience it. I can envision a possible world in
which I place Margaret Thatcher, and then I imagine
what she would have done. Margaret Thatcher is, as it
were, pinned once and for all to a rigid designator; she is
attached to the fishing hook of her proper name, which
is why we can use our imagination to vary her deeds in
possible worlds in which she might have been around.
Whenever we introduce a proper name, we dip our fishing rod, so to speak, into reality. The object for which
we are fishing is attached to our fishing rod, even when
we have false representations about this object or when
we wish we had caught another object (for example,
Gisele Bündchen or Brad Pitt).

From this we see that the *logical identity* of Margaret
Thatcher over possible worlds has very little to do with

the *material identity* of her body at some point in her biological life in the universe. We can always speak about the same Margaret Thatcher as we would have done thirty years ago, even though she no longer has the same material identity (the particles of her former body are spread out by now). Indeed, this is the way it works with all of us. I would still be the same Markus Gabriel if I had eaten sea bream instead of Rhenish roast beef for dinner last night, although today I would consist of different elementary particles.

On top of this, Hilary Putnam added a simple yet witty remark to the thrust of Kripke's argument, namely, that it cannot be the case that I am identical to my elementary particles, because otherwise I would have already existed before my birth, insofar as I would already have been distributed in a different way in the universe. The elementary particles of which I consist existed already before I existed, only in different combinations. If I were identical with them (my elementary particles), I would have existed long before my birth. While we are not logically identical to our bodies, it does not follow that we can exist without bodies. Kripke's and Putnam's arguments only prove that we cannot be logically identical with elementary particles, such that many objects exist which cannot be ontologically reduced to existing in the universe. For this reason, materialistic monism is false because there are many objects (for example, us as persons) whose logical identity differs from their material realization.

Unfortunately the scientific worldview is joined up with many bad fairy tales. Willard Van Orman Quine, one of the strictest disciples of the scientific worldview, even finds it necessary at one point in his considerations to describe his scientific worldview itself as a fairy tale (as he puts it, as "myth"). At a much quoted point in his very influential essay "Two Dogmas of Empiricism," Quine compares the assumption of physical objects (such as electrons) with the assumption that Homer's gods exist:

Let me interject that for my part I do, qua lay physicist, believe in physical objects and not in Homer's gods; and I consider it a scientific error to believe otherwise. But in point of epistemological footing the physical objects and the gods differ only in degree and not in kind. Both sorts of entities enter our conception only as cultural posits. The myth of physical objects is epistemologically superior to most in that it has proved more efficacious than other myths as a device for working a manageable structure into the flux of experience.[44]

Quine is a very genuine materialist. For he assumes that knowledge, if anything, is itself a material process in which information arising as a result of our nerve endings receiving stimulation through contact with the physical environment is assimilated. Accordingly, any theory has to be constructed by way of complicated interpretations of stimuli. General concepts (such as cause, effect, elementary particles) are a variety of helpful fictions which we use in order to make sense of our nerve stimulations. From this it follows, however, that the hypothesis itself at some level appears to be random. Quine arbitrarily manipulates his nerve stimulations into a worldview. However, in so doing he commits a mistake, which should be avoided in a scientific age: he chooses between worldviews the one that he likes best, because it can be most easily described mathematically. By the same law one could turn back to Homer's gods and describe these mathematically (which would be even easier to do because, depending on the total count, one has to deal only with twelve gods).

The Book of the World

Quine's description of how we acquire knowledge in a world that is completely material loses sight of reality as we experience it. Putnam – who was Quine's colleague at Harvard – has emphasized that we should not think of scientific knowledge as based on the construction of myths.[45] In this connection Putnam argues against Quine for a SCIENTIFIC REALISM, according to which the sciences discover what exists in their domain of objects and do not simply posit this content themselves. If it is true that electrons exist, then electrons are no mere "cultural posits," but electrons. Though they are themselves not directly observable, elementary particles must actually exist in the object domain of physics. They are not merely useful hypotheses, but objects which are integrated into facts subject to scientific investigation.

A similar principle *mutatis mutandis* applies to every true statement, irrespective of the particular science from which it may be derived. If it is true that Goethe is the author of *Faust*, then this is not a useful fiction of German studies. After all, we do not invent the author named "Goethe" in order to make our interpretation easier. Goethe once existed and he really was the author of *Faust*. At first, not much follows from this. Yet the trivial insight that Goethe wrote *Faust* is a fact about Goethe and not about our model of reality. Goethe is not a building block in a worldview, but a historical person who lived during a certain period of time on the European continent, where he wrote *Faust*.

At this point it would probably be helpful to refer back to the constructivist position, which is closely connected to talk of "worldviews." Although it exists in diverse variations, the following consideration always appears to be the basis of one or another version of constructivism: let us imagine a green apple. In our worldview green apples exist. Now let us introduce a wasp, which flies around the apple. Does the wasp also see a green apple? The wasp sees a different color spectrum than we do; after all, it has compound eyes. Maybe it does not see an apple at all. Isn't it then naïve on our part simply to suppose that there are green apples? Is this not a very provincial way of looking at reality? In addition, let us also introduce a dolphin, who receives a sonar representation of the object that we see as a green apple. Don't we all – namely, humans, the wasp, and the dolphin – see (or "sonar") only our own world, our own object, without ever being able to determine how things are constituted in themselves? Isn't belief in an objective world always based on interpretations of nerve irritations? But if this applies to our sensory impressions, doesn't it also apply to the natural sciences because, even while in principle in the sciences we trust our sensory impressions, we employ instruments in experiments? In order to use any instrument whatsoever, we need to rely on our sensory impressions. Against this background, constructivism infers that each sees only his own world, but never the thing in itself.

In contrast, REALISM claims that, if we ever know anything at all, we know things in themselves. And SCIENTIFIC REALISM is the corresponding thesis that, by virtue of our experimentally confirmed theories and scientific hardware, we know things in themselves, not merely our constructs.

New realism intends to redeem a program that has already cropped up once before under the same name but at the time was not capable of being substantiated.[46] For, above all, it is only through philosophers in the second half of the twentieth century (most notably Michael Dummett and Hilary Putnam) that essential progress in the elaboration of realism was attained. In the history of philosophy, many different suggestions have been offered regarding how one should actually understand the term "realism" and which theses can best be connected with it. As with all other concepts, one understands philosophical concepts in the clearest way only when one sees their contrast. For our purposes, the most important contrasting concept to realism is not idealism, as some readers may presume, but nominalism – an important forerunner of modern constructivism.

NOMINALISM claims that our concepts and categories do not describe or picture structures or divisions of the world as it is in itself but, rather, all concepts which we human beings form about our environment or ourselves are only useful abstractions and generalizations which may be carried out in order to increase our chance of survival. There is actually no universal concept of a horse that covers all horses, but only a plurality of individual things which we simply call "horse" in order to simplify the given phenomena. In the end, concepts are simply empty names, from which nominalism also acquired its name – "nomen" is the Latin word for "name." If our concepts were only generalizations – in themselves empty simplifications usefully unifying all of the various phenomena such as planets, horses, or proteins – we could no longer assume that objects themselves have any kind of structure at all. For no structure that we might impute to the objects would really be able to articulate how they are, as any structure we can make sense of is already conceptual. As an example we can appeal to the structure of a red apple. The apple is red, which means that it is colored. It belongs to the structure of the apple that it is colored. Otherwise it could not be red. Now there exist other colored objects, such as green apples. From this it immediately follows that the object has a structure which other objects can also have. In this sense, its structure is in itself general; it does not apply only to this one object. If all structures were mere abstractions and empty generalizations, expressed in empty, albeit useful words without substance, we could as a consequence no longer presuppose that red and green apples exist.

In general, realism assumes that some of our concepts to which abstract concepts such as love, governments, or the notion of the abstract concept belong are not merely names designed to help us survive. Structures exist; they are real, and we track them conceptually. Against this background, the American philosopher Theodore Sider justifiably defends the thesis that realism in general boils down to the recognition that structures really exist. He introduces this position, STRUCTURAL REALISM, in his book *Writing the Book of the World*, where he calls it a "knee-jerk realism," because it is actually quite difficult to grasp exactly how someone could seriously dispute this position.[47] In general, then, realism is the thesis that there are structures entirely independent of our imagination. While in the end Sider himself advances a monism that is quite materialistic and fairly gratuitous, new realism advances the double thesis, firstly, that we can know things and facts in themselves and, secondly, that things and facts in themselves do not belong to a single domain of objects. Material objects are not the only entities that exist, as there are also logical laws and human knowledge which we can recognize in the same way as material objects. My own version of new realism is field of sense ontology, which claims that all that we know appears in fields of sense. Accordingly, new realism no longer shapes the concept of reality and the concept of knowledge with a view to materialistic monism. In the field of ontology, materialistic monism limps sadly behind the whole history of philosophy, since the theory was first refuted with particularly good arguments by Plato, in his dialogues the *Sophist* and *Parmenides*, and even more explicitly in Aristotle's *Metaphysics*.

In a newspaper article in the *Frankfurter Allgemeine Zeitung* of 4 April 2012, Thomas Thiel reported on the first international conference organized on the theme of "new realism" in Germany. In this article, Thiel raised the question as to whether my approach could prove more than that we know a single thing in itself, namely the fact that there really are facts. If we are able to know only that there are indeed facts, then very little of constructivism's terrain would have been disputed. For in the end it could be the case that we are only ever able to know a single thing, or a single fact, which would indeed be very little. The rest (including green apples and electrons) might still be constructed. Should everything, excluding the position of constructivism itself, prove to be a construction, constructivism could justifiably claim its victory.

In order to see that this is not the case, and that we necessarily know very many facts exactly as they are in themselves, we must once more go back to constructivism's most cherished argument. We will see that the real ground of the argument can be covered much better by new realism. Actually, the alleged argument for constructivism does not really speak in its favor. Thus, the main argument for constructivism does not achieve what it ought to do.

The argument appeals to the physiology of the human senses, and different versions of it were already quite widespread in ancient Greek philosophy.[48] The difference between the ancient Greek and contemporary versions lies simply in the fact that today we know considerably more about the physiology of the human senses (which, however, does not play an important role in the argument itself). The argument begins with the establishment of an obvious fact: everything that we know about the physical surroundings of our body we know insofar as we process information, which is related to the stimulation of our nerve endings.

The things which we see, hear, smell, and feel are always the way they appear to be because we register them in a specific way. Typically the supposed problem resulting from this is illustrated with reference to the sense of vision, which is especially important for human beings. Let us imagine that we see an apple in a fruit bowl. In this case, photons strike the surface of our eyeballs. The electromagnetic radiation to which we are exposed is translated into electric impulses, which in turn are manufactured into a visual picture by our brain. Although everything is completely dark within our skulls, the electric impulses produce stimuli that our visual cortex perceives as pictures. Philosophers call such pictures "mental representations." If all of this is correctly described (which it isn't!), we might come to believe that what we actually see is not really the apple in the fruit bowl, but a mental representation. The view that we never really perceive things as they are in themselves, but actually only mental representations, is called MENTAL REPRESENTATIONALISM. According to this view, we do not literally see the apple in the fruit bowl, but instead we sit in the darkness within our skull, where a film of the world is projected onto a stage created and maintained by electric impulses. This film helps us to orient ourselves in the external world, which in reality consists only of colorless elementary particles and things consisting of a combination of these particles on a higher macroscopic level. If we could look at the things in themselves through "God's eyes," as it were, the situation would appear somewhat terrifying. Where we previously perceived an apple, we would perceive simply vibrating elementary particles or waves of some kind. Nonetheless, that would not be enough, for we would see neither an apple nor our body with its skull. In particular we would no longer be able to recognize the mental representation, the visual picture. This image is therefore the same kind of illusion produced by our brains or, rather, the fundamental particles, as an olfactory representation, an auditory representation, an electro-representation of an elephantnose fish or the sonar representation of a dolphin. For our brains are also only elements in our film. We perceive our brains through our ability to process information. If we never perceive things as they really are, we might start believing that we do not really have brains after all. Brains are mental representations, just like apples.

However, how do we then know that we really do have brains? How do we know how the physiology of the senses functions? Is our only access to our brains and the physiology of our senses through our senses? If we can know something about the external world only by perceiving it through our five senses (in a relevant combination), then this applies also to our knowledge both of the physiology of our senses and of our brain. For we only ever see our brain in a mirror or with the help of a complicated technical registry, but we never pull back and look within our skull in order to determine what is happening there in the darkness of the brain. If all elements that show up on the screen of our consciousness are illusions, then the brain is also only an illusion. If the world or the external world is only a construction formed from sense data, then this thesis is also a construction formed from sense data. Everything disappears into the abyss of a huge (illusory) maelstrom. In this scenario it is not just that we fail to know the thing in itself, but also that anything that we thought we knew was an illusion all along. For mental representationalism, neither brains nor mental representations exist. All of these objects turn out to be mere illusions.

This effective (if somewhat crude) argumentative weapon that can be deployed against mental representationalism, as well as constructivism, is grounded on the physiology of the senses and can be reinforced with a more subtle argument. If constructivism grounded on the physiology of the senses were true, then all objects in our field of sense would be illusions. For this reason, there would no longer be a difference between a hallucination and a normal perception. It no longer makes any difference whether I *see* an apple or *hallucinate* an apple. For even the apple which is seen would in the end be only a kind of hallucination, which the brain (or whoever or whatever it may be) creates through the stimulation of nerve endings (or stimulations of whatever it may be). No instrument of scientific measurement fares any better – they are all hallucinations. For this reason, one can no longer distinguish between true and false mental representations. They are all true insofar as they all arise by virtue of the stimulation of nerve endings, and they are all false insofar as none of the pictures portrays things in themselves. In real life and in the service of naked survival we gladly differentiate with more than average success between hallucinations and the real things that we perceive. This means that, in the end, the supposedly homogeneous field of vision within our skull is in fact not homogeneous at all. Indeed, the content of a mental representation is not an indifferent matter at all. If I perceive a green apple, then a green apple is lying there.* On the contrary, if I hallucinate, or if I "see" a colored afterimage on a white wall after I have stared at the sun, no green apple is lying there. Moreover, in this case there is no afterimage located on the white wall.

If we in fact perceive that an apple is lying in the fruit bowl, then we perceive an apple in the fruit bowl, not its visual image. This is supported by the fact that any number of people are able to see the same apple. Of course it will appear differently to different people, but that does not matter for the fact that there is an apple in the fruit bowl.

In overreaction to the absurdity of mental representationalism, it is all too tempting to return to metaphysics and look for some fundamental level of reality. It now looks as if there must be things in themselves that appear

---

* The term for "perceive" in German is "wahrnehmen," which is a compound of "wahr" (true) and "nehmen" (to take). To perceive is "to take something to be true."

to people in different ways. I can feel, taste, smell, see, and hear (for example, when I clap) my left hand. Thus, one might think there must be a thing in itself, my left hand, that is different from its diverse appearances.

Against this return to metaphysics, new realism simply points out that my left hand cannot be different from the way that it appears. Right now I see my hand from this perspective, and at some other time I see it from another point of view. Whether I see it from here or from there, why should I infer from this either that I do not have a hand at all, or that my hand is completely external to these points of view? The import is that things in themselves appear in different ways. The appearances are themselves things in themselves; they are as real as it gets. The way the appearances exist is contingent upon the field of sense in which they appear. The plurality of ways of appearing is not an illusion hovering over a metaphysical reality always somewhat beyond the ken of our senses. Reality consists not in hard facts lying behind the appearances, but in things in themselves *and* their appearances. How my left hand appears to me is just as real as my left hand itself, and it tells me something about my left hand, namely that it looks this way when seen from here. Things in themselves always appear only in fields of sense, and that means that they are already embedded in facts. Even when we see an afterimage or hallucinate a green apple, we deal in facts, such as the fact that we are hallucinating a green apple. To hallucinate a green apple does not mean that the very hallucination of the green apple is itself a hallucination. Hallucinations are real. The problem is that we might mistake the reality of a hallucination for the reality of a perception.

Against this background, new realism claims that all true knowledge is knowledge of a thing in itself (or a fact in itself). True knowledge is no hallucination or illusion, but an appearance of the matter itself.

Still, might one want to retort in the following way: Isn't the form of vision or the form of taste only a kind of projection, or at least a filter, through which things in themselves appear to us in a potentially or actually distorted way? Let us assume that we see that the apple is lying in the fruit bowl. We differentiate it from the bowl by virtue of its current spatial position. But how do we know that the apple is really, in itself, different from the bowl? Would the difference not be there at all if the spatial differentiation were not recognizable, if we were not to differentiate them spatially? This is exactly how Kant saw the matter, on account of which he was led to the absurd consequence that things in themselves are not even spatial or temporal. It suddenly appears as though the moon can be differentiated from the earth only because we make it so by bringing our specific registries with us.

> We have therefore wanted to say that all our intuition is nothing but the representation of appearance; that the things that we intuit are not in themselves what we intuit them to be, nor are their relations so constituted in themselves as they appear to us; and that if we remove our own subject or even only the subjective constitution of the senses in general, then all constitution, all relations of objects in space and time, indeed space and time themselves, would disappear, and as appearances they cannot exist in themselves, but only in us.[49]

A lot of the things Kant writes in this passage are deeply dubious: What does it mean that space and time can exist "only in us"? Isn't "in us," for example, a specification of place and thereby spatial? Isn't "us," for instance, temporal and doesn't it mean us as we existed yesterday, exist today, and hopefully will still exist tomorrow?

Subjective Truths

Constructivism is absurd, though it does not wear its absurdity on its sleeve, which is why it is still so widespread among both natural and social scientists. We have become accustomed to the notion that everything around us ought to be understood as a hidden cultural construction. At best, the natural sciences might still describe things as they are, but even they have to tarry with *The Hidden Reality*, as the title of Brian Greene's most recent book suggests.[50] This certainly places the so-called humanities in a difficult position. For if they have to do only with cultural constructs, the difference between true and false disappears, and the interpretation of a poem or a historical matter of fact also turns into some kind of hallucination. The motto of the happy constructivist is as follows: to each his own *Faust* or his own November revolution! Everything becomes merely a question of perception.

In *Writing the Book of the World*, which we have already mentioned, Ted Sider suggested a rather accurate diagnosis, which at one go makes new realism reconcilable with constructivism. To this end we can modify Sider's favorite example somewhat. Let us begin with an extremely simplified world that consists of two precisely differentiated halves, of which one is black and the other white.

In this world, which I call "the Sider world" (see figure 6), only a few facts obtain: the fact that two halves exist, one of which is black and the other white, and the fact of their respective magnitudes. Now Sider describes expressions which structurally correspond to facts of the world as "carving nature at its joints." Let's look, for example, at the statements

In the Sider world two halves exist

Figure 6 The Sider world

and

The left half is white, and the right half is black.

Both statements track differences along the joints of the Sider world. Now we can also invent a diagonal language, as I would like to call it. A diagonal language can be achieved with the help of the American philosopher Nelson Goodman.[51] As an example let us introduce the property of being "whack" – that is, part white and part black. We can then cut out a rectangle diagonally from the Sider world that is indeed whack and put forward the following true statement:

This rectangle is whack.

It is easy to come up with many DIAGONAL PREDICATES – that is, with predicates that run diagonally across the Sider world. For the sake of illustration, let us imagine that we cut a diagonal rectangle out of the Sider world that lies in part on the white half and in part on the black half (see figure 7).

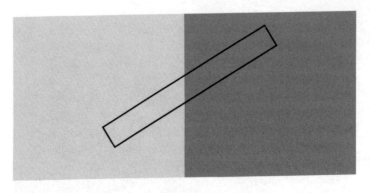

Figure 7

The rectangle cut out of the Sider world can be described as "whack" because every object is "whack" by definition, insofar as it is partly black and partly white. In the diagonal language, there are the predicates "black," "white," and "whack." Goodman, who was one of the main representatives of constructivism in the United States, introduced diagonal predicates in order to show that all predicates are equally good, as long as we presuppose that they make true statements possible. If the function of predicates is to serve in true statements, there is nothing wrong with diagonal languages. And how do we really know which elements of our language are diagonal? Might not most if not all of our language deep down be diagonal? It is an obvious truth about the rectangle that it is whack – and nevertheless we have a sense that "whack" is an inadequate predicate. Sider is completely justified in his insistence that there is a difference between "black" and "whack": "black" is a proper perception of a structure of the Sider world, while "whack" is a human projection.

This becomes even clearer if we introduce another diagonal predicate that makes true statements possible but is completely inadequate:

X is a cat or a moon.

The objects which are cats are differentiated from the objects that are either cats or moons. One can transcribe this in the diagonal language by introducing a new predicate:

X is a catmoon.

On this basis we can easily construct theories about cats, moons, and catmoons. Despite this, we have to reckon that there is a fundamental difference between *normal* and *diagonal* predicates. Sider infers from similar considerations that not all objects mesh with all other objects. Electrons mesh with electrons but not with cats, on account of which we justifiably have no word for "electrats."

Predicates such as "whack," "catmoon," or "electrat" are completely arbitrary, although they make true statements possible. For in the diagonal domain there are "whack" objects and beings, and we can say true things about "electrats," etc.

Against this background it is possible to see how new realism is reconcilable with a dose of acceptable constructivism. All we need is the notion that there really are many quite arbitrary and loony constructions (Vladimir Putin today is quite good at formulating constructions of this type), which even includes the fact that they make true statements possible. Having said that, it is a hopeless overgeneralization to suspect on the basis of this that everything is, or even only might be, a construction or a loony formation.

With further assistance from Sider, one can also differentiate between *diagonal language* and *human subjectivity*. A diagonal language only answers to our need for capriciousness; it allows us to introduce truth-conferring predicates in any way we wish, and in so doing design different language games. In contradistinction to mere diagonality one can now introduce SUBJECTIVE PREDICATES, which are not subjective in the sense of being private – that is, only my or your predicates – but instead predicates shared by all subjects of a certain community. To this might belong the following predicate:

X is a beautiful spring morning.

People experience certain spring mornings as beautiful. Our sense of a beautiful spring morning, our feeling of spring, may be grounded in the history of our species. It could be objectively studied to the extent to which it holds on account of our animal nature. Yet the predicate of beautiful spring mornings on another level does not cut nature along its joints. Subjective but non-diagonal predicates could, for example, be represented by a black circle which we cut out of the right half of the rectangle. Such a circle would still fall short of a joint of the world independent of spectators, but it would nevertheless not be a loony construction (see figure 8).

The upshot of this discussion is that there are many subspecies of constructions, illusions, and truths, as well as of capriciousness. Constructivism oversimplifies matters insofar as it assumes only one single form of appearance and explains this as a product of different kinds of brains or of various human languages or socioeconomic factors.

Against this, new realism posits that there exist subjective truths – that is, truths which are accessible only if certain registers are in play – that our human subjectivity or different forms of human or more general animal subjectivity make possible. From this it follows neither that subjective forms are a kind of arbitrary hallucination or that they are false in some way, nor that one cannot know things along their joints as they are in themselves.

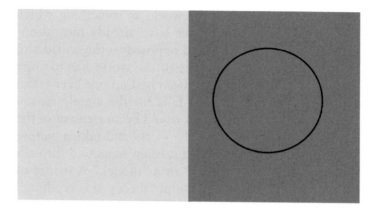

Figure 8

Holzwege*

Constructivism is up to no good in almost all regions of human knowledge and science. Whenever we come upon the concept of a "worldview," we must assume that we are in constructivism's zone of influence. Heidegger identified this problem in his essay "The Age of the World Picture":

> Hence world picture, when understood essentially, does not mean a picture of the world but the world conceived and grasped as picture. What is, in its entirety, is now taken in such a way that it first is in being and only is in being to the extent that it is set up by man, who represents and sets forth.[52]

---

* As is well known, "Holzwege" is the title of an essay by Heidegger that is notoriously difficult to translate, for which reason the term has been left in the original German. The idiomatic expression in which it appears, "auf dem Holzweg sein," means something like "to bark up the wrong tree," "to go up a blind alley," or "to be on the wrong track." The term literally means "lumber (Holz) path (Weg)," a logging path. When hiking in the forest, for instance, one may by accident take a wrong turn onto a logging path, a path that leads to a clearing in the forest. The Cambridge edition of "Holzwege," edited and translated by Julian Young and Keith Hayes, has the title *Off the Beaten Track*.

Whenever we represent the world as something which we can take a picture of, we have already metaphorically assumed that we stand opposed to the world and that the picture that we take of the world has to copy the world as it would have been had no one ever taken a picture. Yet this analogy fails for the simple reason that the picture of the world would be an element of the world, as we cannot leave the world and take a picture from outside. The same idea is often suggested through the expression of a "theory" or a "model." A theory of the world in the sense of a literal "theory of everything" cannot exist for many reasons. The simplest reason, to which Heidegger alluded, lies in the fact that the world is not the object of a representation. We do not look at the world from outside the world, which would enable us to ask whether our worldview is adequate. If this were so, it would be as if one wanted to take a picture of everything – including the camera. But this is impossible. For, if the camera showed up in our picture, then the photographed camera would not be identical to the camera taking the photograph, just as my image in the mirror is not completely identical with who I am. Every worldview remains, at the very least, a worldview from inside the world – that is to say, a picture of the world from the middle of things, a picture, therefore, that slightly alters the world by taking place within it.

Besides, we already know that this move misses the matter at hand. For the world, the total domain, the field of sense of all fields of sense, does not exist and cannot exist. For this reason the basic idea of a worldview is absurd. All worldviews are off the beaten track, because they want to be pictures of something that does not exist. In the best-case scenario, one has only ever taken a picture of a part of the world, which typically leads to a one-sided representation that is prematurely generalized.

Constructivism set out from the apparently quite

natural and correct assumption that we build theories or models. These are considered as though they are like nets, which we lay over the world in order to determine to what extent the world has become caught up in them. Yet this imagery overlooks a very simple thought which is at the center of new realism: the argument from facticity.[53]

FACTICITY means that there is something rather than nothing – that is, that there exists anything at all. The argument from facticity objects against constructivism that it overlooks this, namely that it fails to acknowledge that constructions themselves are things that really exist. It cannot be the case that constructions are constructed, for why then would we ever have a reason to stop and accept that there are any constructions? In order for constructivism to be about constructions and not, for example, about bananas, a few things must hold good: it must be a theory which contains assertions, in particular the assertion that all theories are constructed. Within these parameters constructivism typically claims that some quantity of facts exist relative to some epistemic system or other, whether this be a system of belief, a registry, or a particular formal structure. Thus, in general it claims:

All the facts F are relative to some epistemic system S.

Neuroconstructivism, for example, claims that the colorful world that appears to us is relative to the specificity of the human organism, our brain in particular. It asserts that, if there were no brains of a specific kind, then it would not be true that I am currently sitting – once again – in the train from Aarhus to Copenhagen and that I have been traveling by dark green meadows and yellow rapeseed fields for the past twenty minutes. If during the composition of these lines all the brains in the universe had disappeared, the sentence would have been false according to constructivism – there would not have been a train traveling by dark green meadows, as colors would never have come into existence. HERMENEUTICAL CONSTRUCTIVISM, a constructivism that concerns the interpretation of texts, similarly maintains that *Faust* does not have any interpretation independent of its readers. Whether witches exist in *Faust* would be a fact that obtains only relative to a particular interpretation.

Now we can ask the simple question whether there can be a universal constructivism – that is, a constructivism that renders all facts relative to an epistemic system. We sometimes encounter people who claim in an undifferentiated way that *everything* is relative, or people who think that we can build only largely insufficient pictures, models, or theories of the world. In this case all facts pertaining to constructivism would obviously be relative to a system. However, this would mean that we would end up with the following nested situation of an infinite fact:

$$\{[(T \text{ is relative to } S) \text{ is relative to } S] \text{ is relative to } S\} \text{ is relative to } S \ldots$$

In this model there can be nothing to which everything is relative. Everything is relative, but it is not the case that everything is relative to some final system, as the final system could consist of facts only if these facts, in turn, were relevant to a further system. The infinite chain of relative entities hangs, as it were, in the air. Nonetheless, universal constructivism ought to be the thesis that everything is relative. But if it follows from this that there is nothing to which everything is relative, the result is a single fact infinitely nested within itself. However, then there would only be one fact, namely that there is only one fact that is infinitely nested within itself! At this point it is unclear what the universal constructivist had in mind when he proposed that everything was relative.

The insight that constructivism is false for all the reasons mentioned thus far is the insight into how things are in themselves. When we think about facts philosophically and catalogue successful results, we know facts that are just as objective as the difference between cats and mattresses or proteins and protons. The falsity of universal constructivism, or the manifold problematic assumptions built into the idea that reality as it is in itself does not contain colors, tells us something about how things really are, and this is brought out by philosophy.

The argument from facticity underpins a general *realism about reason itself*, according to which human reason itself has a factual structure which we can investigate scientifically, whereby we discover something about how things really are. The "external world" or nature or the "universe" are no longer privileged domains of facts when it comes to our grasp of what it means for something to exist. Put simply: if I think the true thought that it is raining, then two facts exist: first, the fact that it is raining and, second, the fact that I think the true thought that it is raining. Consequently, facts find themselves not only on the "side of the world," as the scientific worldview tends to assume, but also on the side of those who comport themselves towards facts on the "side of the world." And, even if there were no material objects, there would be facts – for example, the fact that there are no material objects. Facticity is inescapable and so is truth. Facts do not go away simply because we do not look at them. Yet the reason for this cannot be found in the material universe, since, regardless of whether or not we acknowledge it, this is neither the privileged nor the only domain of facts that exists. For this reason, the argument from facticity comes to the conclusion that we cannot get around facticity. In any situation there will always be non-constructed facts in play. Our task is to recognize what these facts consist in.

By the way, in our everyday life we are all at least implicitly committed to the realism of reason itself. Let us imagine ourselves once again in a completely commonplace situation. It is lunchtime, and we are wondering what to eat in the cafeteria. In order to answer this question, we weigh the various options: because I already ate fish yesterday and anyway the fish from the cafeteria is usually an unhealthy slab of fried fish, I should go for the salad bar today; above all, the bratwurst should be avoided. Thus, I put a salad plate together, and I select something from what I find at hand. On my way to the salad bar I meet a colleague, Ms "So and so," from the "Such and such" department, I receive a phone call, and I think about going home after work. All these are facts at the joints of the field of sense of lunchtime, and every single bit of knowledge obtained is knowledge of things or facts in themselves. I thereby assume that my thoughts are facts arising in accordance with further facts: I treat my thoughts as real, which is quite natural for conscious creatures leading a pretty rational life. In a lunchtime situation no one seriously believes that elementary particles are more real or more factual than the thoughts that we create or the colors of the salad bar. As a consequence, the privileging of particular facts in the name of realism is ungrounded and erroneous. For this reason new realism insists on an investigation of what exists that is without bias. We should not allow any traditionally received worldview, whether this be ancient or modern, to determine what is "real" or what "exists," just because alleged authorities such as "religion" or "science" have sanctioned this. A lot is true which cannot be investigated by the natural sciences, such as the question as to whether everything that exists could be investigated by the natural sciences! Furthermore, even in the natural sciences there are quite fanciful diagonal predicates, which are eliminated with scientific progress. Sigmund Freud points this out in his book *The Joke and its Relation to the Unconsciousness* with a joke that he ascribes to Georg Christoph Lichtenberg. In a well-known passage Hamlet says: "There are more things in heaven and earth, Horatio, than are dreamt of in your philosophy"[54] – a classical critique of the scientific worldview. To this, Freud reminds us, we ought to add: "But there is also much in philosophy which is found neither in heaven nor on earth."[55]

Science and Art

The scientific worldview assumes a specific view of the human being. According to this view, the idealized scientist is a thoroughly rational thinker. The production of knowledge is ideally as follows. The scientist encounters an unknown phenomenon, such as a disease, and formulates a hypothesis. He subsequently justifies or rejects this hypothesis through a methodologically controlled process, in which every single step is repeatable and is comprehensible to all other scientists. The founding father of this method is Descartes, who suggested that we doubt everything in our lives at least once and, from there, establish a new science that is rationally justified. Then, in an idealized scientific method, one should develop a worldview via a completely neutral hypothesis. Every step to be taken has to result from this completely neutral position, the Zero of knowledge. However, such a position is a fiction as well as an ideal: we will always have to take something for granted that is unjustified, and even unjustifiable, in light of the theories we subsequently develop.

The Cartesian ideal driving our conception of science to the present time approaches science and rational thought as if every single one of our beliefs was a hypothesis that could be tested scientifically. Yet most of our beliefs are not of this kind. For instance, when we are on a date and are convinced that our opposite number is slowly falling in love with us, we do not formulate a scientific hypothesis and then methodologically appraise whether this is the case (well, perhaps one could do this, but presumably only once, as such an examination would threaten the success of the absolute majority of all dates). Similar considerations apply to political or aesthetic situations. This does not scare off the current generation of researchers from investigating such domains of human life as if they were, say, events in our brains.

It has been proposed that the neural processes accompanying our appreciation of artworks should be investigated in order to determine what good art is. This assumes an untenable form of constructivism, as it makes the quality of art entirely dependent upon our contingent sensory factors of appreciation, as if art were generally simply a matter of pattern recognition, an actualization of habits naturally selected that happened to be helpful in our earlier survival struggle in the animal kingdom. Understanding *Hamlet*, Proust's *In Search of Lost Time*, a Beethoven symphony, or the development of Picasso's work over several periods, however, is not some kind of elaborate IQ test, where some of us would just be better at recognizing shapes or number series. Even the idea that the meaning of a work of art is to be sought solely in the fact that we find it beautiful should be rejected, at the very least because it might lead to the misguided notion that we find it beautiful since certain nerve stimulations are triggered in viewers, readers, or listeners. Such views date back to the eighteenth century and were refuted by almost all work in the field of the manifold theories dealing with art in its various ramifications in the nineteenth and twentieth century. In a similar light, one could, of course, investigate specific color patterns, or the patterns underlying the phenomenon of apparent movement without which we humans could not watch films, and figure out how all of this is related to hard-wired structures in our nervous system. Yet none of this would contribute anything to an understanding of, say, the stylistic features in Jean-Luc Godard or Terry Gilliam. Figuring out how apparent movement is related to hard-wired structures in our brain may indeed be useful for some purpose, but it does not really enhance our understanding of works of art. If anything, whether or not we like a specific painting from Picasso's Blue Period, whether it is physically appealing to us, whether we feel good when we view it, plays a subordinate role for the actual meaning of his work from this period. (The idea that this might be what understanding an artwork boils down to is, by the way, a notion that is undermined by modern art by virtue of its aesthetic of ugliness and deformity.) In order to understand Picasso, what is required is a combination of knowledge of art history, creative imagination, and openness to new interpretations. On this level, the fact that one also needs a brain to understand Picasso is as relevant for our understanding of his work as the fact that one needs a good night's sleep or that one could take a bus or a taxi or go on foot to the art gallery. In general, it would not be too hard to establish the thesis that at every possible opportunity modern art proves to be against the scientific worldview. Almost every aesthetic movement and every single artist repudiates the position that artistic production can in the end be reduced to natural scientific processes. For instance, many of Jeff Koons's hyper-pop culture objects could not have been created without technological progress having been made. Such objects are a result of technology being pushed to its limits in combination with the artist's creative imagination. In order to flesh out my point a little bit more, let us take a look at one of Jackson Pollock's "action paintings," for example *Number 8* from 1949.

At first sight one might think that it consists merely of paint-splatter on a colored background. If this exhausted the meaning of this painting, all of Pollock's works in this phase would amount to the same; one could at most have a subjective opinion and say which picture one likes the best, without this being anything more than the expression of one's current state of mind. One could then objectify this a bit by employing neuroscientific methods to investigate the causal background of one's feelings. Yet all of this completely misses Pollock's point. Action paintings are not just action, they are also real paintings. This means, in particular, that they have a highly specific dynamic and can be interpreted in complex and manifold ways. In order to *understand* an "action painting" (and not merely to find it beautiful) one can follow a particular color and read it from left to right. One might concentrate, for example, on the color black and follow its tracks. By doing so the total impression begins to flicker, and the black dots and random lines become meaningful and begin to move. Now one might shift one's perspective and follow the color green – or accentuate the background and read the picture in other directions. One might proceed in the same way in order to unlock a classical figurative painting. Every painting is also colors on a canvas, so ordered that its meaning is revealed. Understanding a painting involves understanding the dynamic of color as an expression of artistic intention, which is typically assumed and made explicit by Pollock.

Pollock has thereby produced a meta-painting, as it were, which shows us how we actually proceed when we read a work of art: we follow the contours of its colors and move across the various levels to understand the meaning and consider various interpretations, for which we appeal to our background knowledge of art history and spontaneous insights, which we then discuss with others. Pollock's paintings thereby confront us with our actions, our intentions to understand the works. They are also action paintings in the sense in which they reveal the action of the artist to the action of understanding it. This process of understanding is in no way completely arbitrary, but it is free. The freedom of understanding works of art consists in the fact that we simultaneously understand something and experience the way that we understand it. Understanding an artwork involves confrontation with our assumptions regarding what it is to understand something. By the way, this is the upshot of philosophical hermeneutics as conceived by the German philosopher Hans-Georg Gadamer: artworks reveal features of our understanding and thereby contribute to self-understanding.

Understanding personal or political decisions, or a work of art, is neither purely biological nor mathematically describable, nor is it completely arbitrary or merely a matter of taste. It is simply absurd to believe that the meaning of an artwork lies in the eye of the beholder. This view could only be defended by someone who lacks the requirement of art appreciation. The scientific worldview suggests that the meaning of human existence can be passed over in almost all domains, because it believes in a privileged fact structure that is ultimately identical with the universe, the object domain of the natural sciences. Given that the universe does not ask any questions of meaning and does not typically challenge our assumptions of understanding, the simple existence of artworks and of human intentional action is already a mystery to the scientific worldview. Yet, this is only a mystery if one tries to avoid meaning, to reside in a sphere devoid of human presence, a desire encapsulated in the recent nightmarish scenario of "Mars One," a trip to Mars with no return.* As the French singer Camille puts it in a beautiful song of hers: "Mars is no fun."

In their critical rejection of Kant's constructivism, the so-called German idealists (most notably Friedrich Wilhelm Joseph Schelling and Georg Wilhelm Friedrich Hegel) at the beginning of the nineteenth century placed the understanding of meaning at the heart of philosophy. The assumption that there really is meaning to be understood they referred to as SPIRIT [*Geist*], from which the humanities in the German language owe their name.† Spirit in this context does not merely mean something mental or subjective; rather, it signifies the meaning dimension of human understanding. This dimension is investigated by the humanities and, in opposition to a hasty rejection of spirit by postmodern constructivism, is of the utmost importance in rehabilitating spirit. Just because a few French philosophers of the last century, above all Jacques Derrida, were of the opinion that the word "spirit" is a politically suspicious category and indicates a subliminal totalitarianism, there is no reason to be dissuaded from wanting to understand Pollock, Homer, or an episode of *Seinfeld*.[56] There exist different fields of sense which are accessible in different ways and capable of being interpreted in various ways. The study of Romance languages is just as objective and truth-apt as physics or the natural sciences, and necessary if one ever wants to understand Marcel Proust or Italo Calvino. Even in novels there are joints which structure its field of sense, and in the interpretation of a novel we can also be taken in by diagonal predicates. There

* The Mars One Mission aims "to establish a human settlement on Mars," with the first landing scheduled for 2025. See www.mars-one.com/mission (accessed on 17 February 2014).

† The connection between spirit and the humanities is not obvious in English, as it is in German. The humanities, the "Geisteswissenschaften," are literally "the sciences of spirit."

is nothing inherently less real or objective in spirit, as long as one has not decided just to ignore it. Mere spiritlessness (as Kierkegaard has called this) does not make spirit go away but reveals itself in the anxious attempt to explain it away or simply to repress it.

Most fundamentally, the scientific worldview is based on a distorted perception of rationality. It assumes that in all of our efforts to understand we rely upon the construction of hypotheses and the subsequent activity of either proving or discarding them experimentally. Trial-and-error procedures of this type are useful, but they are not appropriate everywhere. They help us to understand the universe. But the human being and our understanding of meaning are not found in the universe; we do not wise up except by drawing nearer to understanding spirit or meaning. This was brought to our attention by the famous Heidelberg philosopher of hermeneutics Hans-Georg Gadamer: "Being that can be understood is language."[57] This much quoted sentence is found in Gadamer's main work *Truth and Method*, in which he shows that the meaning of works of art and the general understanding of the human world is of a completely different kind than our understanding of nature. The human search for truth gets along without method, for there is truth without method (which might have been the better title for the book), which does not mean that it is arbitrary or completely anarchical. It just does not follow the method in the envisaged sense of the vaguely defined "scientific method."

We do not understand our fellow human beings by way of application of the scientific method, which would be a bad choice when it comes to the superior forms of understanding we already employ. For example, try figuring out the neural connections in the brain of a business partner or an entire company or even a country (if you are the prime minister of the United Kingdom, say)! This is, strictly speaking, impossible for

human beings and will never actually be possible. Yet
we can understand people rather well. We are just regularly irritated by the fact of their freedom, which means
precisely that they do not always follow predictable
patterns. How we understand our fellow human beings
is an expression of our personality, and our personality is by no means only a sum of our eating, sleeping,
and mating habits. Personality itself is much more like
a work of art, on account of which modern painting or
modern theatre has long suggested that we are paint-
ers of ourselves. The human being is living creativity.
Creativity, imagination, and originality are signs of
personality, and they can be removed neither from
the humanities nor from the natural sciences. Werner
Heisenberg, one of the greatest and most original scientists of all time, once wrote:

> The spirit of the time is probably a fact just as objective
> as any fact in natural science, and this spirit brings out
> certain features of the world to appearance, which are
> even independent of time and in this sense are eternal.
> The artist tries in his work to make these features under-
> standable, and in this attempt he is led to the forms of
> the style in which he works.
>
> Therefore, the two processes, that of science and that
> of art, are not very different. Both science and art form
> in the course of the centuries a human language by which
> we can speak about the more remote parts of reality, and
> the coherent sets of concepts as well as the different
> styles of art are different words or groups of words in
> this language.[58]

Thus, the failure of the scientific worldview lies not in science per se but in an unscientific conception that deifies
science and brings it into the suspicious neighborhood
of poorly understood religion. This is why contemporary scientistic neo-atheism is a sect: it has faith in a
vaguely defined concept, "science," or "the scientific

method," with a super-object (the universe) answering all questions (if asked in the language of mathematics). We can no longer afford not to understand religion, as we effectively live in an epoch of religious wars. And anyone acquainted with the history of theology over the last five hundred years will be able to see how modernity and its imperatives are largely driven by theological patterns, the details of which have been emphasized by Hans Blumenberg or Peter Sloterdijk. Science does not achieve a worldview, but instead explains just whatever it is able to explain – a molecule, an eclipse of the sun, a line from a novel, or a logical mistake in an argument. The insight that the world does not exist helps us again to draw close to reality and to know that we are people. And people move in spirit. If one ignores spirit and views only the universe, as a matter of course one loses contact with human meaning. That is the fault not of the universe but of ourselves. Modern nihilism is based on an unscientific mistake, namely the mistake of confusing things in themselves with things in the universe and of merely positing that everything else is just a biochemically induced hallucination. One should not acquiesce in this illusion. It is entirely unscientific – at best, science fiction, as in recent movies such as *Her*, *Lucy* or *Transcendence*. Don't get me wrong, I love *Doctor Who* (even though Richard Dawkins once made an appearance in it), but I do not mistake it for an imminent reality that will solve our problems (such as the war in Syria or the conflict in the Middle East more generally).

V

The Meaning of Religion

Philosophy since its inception has been engaged in a scientific way with the question concerning the meaning of the whole. This question is bound up with the question concerning the meaning of human life. Does our life have a meaning which transcends our everyday meaning, the meaning we give to it? Is the meaning that we associate with our life perhaps only a human, all-too-human projection, an illusion which we talk ourselves into, in order to deal with death, evil, and the completely meaningless experiences of pain to which we are exposed?

Philosophy has the task of addressing this question, the question concerning the meaning of human life. For this reason it should not be assumed that we find ourselves in a meaningless material universe, in which we are merely intelligent flesh machines or, in the best-case scenario, killer apes with religious and metaphysical illusions. Yet one cannot just answer straight away the question concerning the meaning of human life – which is obviously interlocked with the meaning of religion. First we must investigate the assumptions upon which modern nihilism is grounded, as it claims that all human meaning is a delusion and makes us believe that we are strangers in a cold universe that stretches out in a meaningless and uninhabited expanse.

When we ask ourselves what it all actually means, we must first zoom out to a maximal distance and view the universe, the world, reality, from above or from the outside, as it were. Recent philosophy, over the last fifty years, has become aware of the fact that such a "bird's-eye view" really corresponds to the fantasy of a "God's-eye point of view," which brings religion into play, for it does indeed appear that God reserves the right to view his creation in this way. Obviously this standpoint is an illusion. Absolute concepts such as "the universe," "the world," and "reality" do not refer to any object at all; they lead us to believe that something exists that does not exist. It is similar to the case of whole numbers: suppose that we begin to look for the biggest whole number. At some point it will hopefully occur to us that the biggest whole number cannot exist, because we can always arrive at a larger number simply by adding 1. So it is with metaphysical concepts of totality: whenever we imagine we are closing in on the super-thing or the super-object, around the next corner of thought there will always be a more comprehensive field of sense.

Giving up on totality for good should trigger the experience of a radical and ultimately free-floating creativity, an infinite freedom. There is always much more than we expected. Fields of sense extend in every possible direction in a way that is endlessly interweaving without being able to determine in advance which rules govern the extension of the fields. If there were a rule that codified which field of sense followed the next, then the world would exist. The world, the whole, would then be the rule which governs everything. But such a rule does not exist and cannot exist. It does not exist for reasons similar to those leading to the insight that the biggest whole number cannot exist.

In the preceding chapter we were confronted with some of the shortcomings of the so-called scientific worldview. It turned out to be a gigantic illusion, which promises us ultimate knowledge from a God's-eye point of view by paradoxically stripping the world of all meaning. This crisis of meaning is often associated with the "disenchantment of the world," as the great sociologist Max Weber called it. In his famous lecture "Science as a Vocation," which he gave in Munich in 1917, Weber does indeed describe modern scientific progress as "intellectual rationalizing through science and scientifically oriented technology."[59] According to Weber, this means that we happen to rely upon an ever increasing division of labor which no single person can actually oversee. The absence of overall governance is then compensated by the fantasy of an ever present eye secretly watching the social sphere. The reality of modern life as a matter of fact is more complex than anything we could ever have imagined. Modernity is almost completely unmanageable and opaque. Nonetheless we assume that it is rational, that the foundations of our social order are secured through scientific procedures, which in principle each one of us can learn and understand. The idea is that everything is in perfect order, an order that one could ascertain if only one had the time and inclination. We have the impression that society is in the hands of experts: management experts, scientific experts, or experts in law. It is precisely this illusory or ideological assumption that Weber calls the "disenchantment of the world":

> The increasing intellectualization and rationalization do *not*, therefore, indicate an increased and general knowledge of the conditions under which one lives. It means something else, namely the knowledge or belief that if one but wished one could learn it at any time. Hence, it means that in principle there are no mysterious incalculable forces that come into play, but rather that one can, in principle, master all things by calculation. This means that the world is disenchanted.[60]

Interestingly, here Weber advances the opposite of what is usually attributed to him. He is not claiming that modernity rests on a lucid and fully transparent disenchanted world governed by autonomous subjects with no respect for religious authorities (where would you find this, by the way, outside of a small academic elite?) but that disenchantment is an illusory self-description accompanying a social process which one can indeed make transparent and investigate with the help of sociology. Accordingly, "disenchantment" does not designate the discovery that the universe is a "cold home." Rather, disenchantment is a social process which manifests on the level of ideology in the form of the belief that we are all part of a rational social order whose rationality consists in the alleged fact that it is governed by some overall set of laws, the laws its individual members have to follow in order to count as rational. This illusion is widespread, and it underlies many general theories about the functioning of our economies or the foundations of political structures. What Weber emphasizes is that the idea of a rule-governed overall social system differentiated into subsystems and subcultures by laws that are similar to the laws of nature is largely theoretically unjustified. Nevertheless, it co-determines the actual course of political events and does not merely accompany it as a form of harmless ivory tower theory-building. To put it another way, our illusions about the workings of the social order as a matter of fact contribute to shaping it. It is part of what a social order is that we relate to it via very broad assumptions about the nature of social action. Rationalization, therefore, is a form of disenchantment only at the level of a certain ideology. We want to make it the case that the social order is rational, which does not thereby simply make it the case that there is a social order corresponding to this idea.

Crucially, disenchantment in this precise sense must

be strictly differentiated from secularization – that is, the replacement of religion by science, in the sense of a replacement of a religious explanation of some phenomenon by a corresponding scientific explanation. Notice that, ironically, Weber calls disenchantment the "fate of our times,"[61] from which one can read what he is really after. He would like to prove that rationalization and disenchantment are not facts which have taken place in modernity and are consummated there, but that disenchantment is a self-description suggested to and by citizens of modern societies, who at the same time cannot see through their own societies. This is why it is their fate. Disenchantment takes place insofar as we assume an underlying rationality of the social order – completely independent of whether it really exists or not. This is why Weber speaks of a faith [Glaube] in rationality. In the end he considers the self-description of modern citizens to be a systematic distortion uncovered by the discipline with which he has been associated ever since: sociology. Ultimately Weber is a sociologist, and sociology investigates objective processes that take place whether we know them or not. At this level it does not differ from the natural sciences. It aims at objective truth about processes that involve subjects with specific beliefs. But that does not make it less objective as a science. One of the differences between the objects studied by the natural sciences and those studied by sociology boils down to the simple fact that social processes do not take place without people – their actions and perceptions – while the earth would revolve around the sun even without us.

Ultimately the process Weber calls "disenchantment" is driven by the modern differentiation of society into its subsystems, a process that no single person, institution or subsystem is capable of overseeing in one glance or with recourse to just one set of rules. The German sociologist Niklas Luhmann has tried to reconstruct this process with his theory of social systems in order to overcome Weber's idea that social action is primarily intentional and rational. Luhmann diagnoses a blind spot in Weber's methodology, but this is another question. Yet what Luhmann points out in the same spirit as Weber is that the assumption of rationality, disenchantment, is part of what, with sociological irony, he calls the "old European" inheritance.

Luhmann refers to this inheritance as the "rationality continuum." What he means is the assumption that there is a single form of rationality which, in principle, dominates the whole world and coincides with its ordering principle – as if the all of reality already lay within the bounds of human rationality. This assumption is ontologically completely indefensible, as we have just shown; it is in fact a burden on us delivered by the history of human thought since the Presocratics, which we must discard, for it is a mistake.

Weber or Luhmann are by no means the only ones who have recognized that there is a modern belief in progress which equips science with virtually magical powers. This attitude is a modern version of fetishism. By FETISHISM, I understand the projection of supernatural powers onto an object that one has actually produced oneself. This projection is conducted in order to integrate one's own identity into a rational whole. Understanding ourselves as a part of a rational whole equips us with a feeling of security, of somehow being at ease with how things are, etc. It is easier for us to live with the thought that things (including social institutions) are by themselves rule-governed than with the thought that we must take care to ensure social cooperation so that the social order does not fall apart. The great whole in which we insert ourselves is at best society itself, whose differentiation we cannot see through. Fetishism consists in projecting this structure onto an object. In fetishism our individual responsibility for our identity, as well as our integration in a social world, which can never fully be controlled, is placed at a distance from us.

The word "fetishism" comes from the Portuguese word *feitiço*, which in turn comes from the Latin "facere," meaning "to make" or "to produce." A "fetish" is an object which one has made in such a way that one fools oneself at the same time into thinking that one has not made it. But, one might wonder, in what respect is the scientific worldview really a form of fetishism? And what does that mean for religion?

The French psychoanalyst Jacques Lacan has introduced the fitting formula that human beings are always searching for a "subject supposed to know," a "sujet supposé savoir." Despite the manifold complications of his theory, his basic idea is quite straightforward and convincing.

Let us place ourselves in a familiar situation. We are sitting on our bicycle at a crosswalk. Pedestrians are standing on the other side. We assume that our actions will coordinate with one another as soon as the light changes to green. For the other users of the road are just as familiar with the rules as we are, and they will attempt to give us enough room to cross the street. This assumption is a requirement of successful street navigation. We would be totally debilitated if we had to expect every user to interpret the rules of the road however they wished or to break the rules as they saw fit. Rather, we follow all kinds of unwritten laws whose regions of application are implicitly always being negotiated anew. The rule, for instance, that cyclists should be cautious towards pedestrians belongs to this class of unwritten laws, because they are riding a powerful and dangerous vehicle made of metal that might injure pedestrians. From this many pedestrians infer that they have every right to make life difficult for cyclists, because in the end they find themselves to be the weaker party. Cyclists play the same game with motorists, such that in reality street traffic appears as a continual debate which, as is well known, commonly enough degenerates into violent arguments in stressful situations in everyday life.

Another instructive example is the supermarket checkout queue and the very different rules of conduct that govern standing in a queue in different societies. In Germany, for instance, in certain supermarkets in residential neighborhoods one pays higher prices, among other things, because the queues are guaranteed to be shorter, and so one's wait is more relaxed. The same products that are available elsewhere at lower prices are made more expensive so that fewer people will shop there. On the other hand, in America there is a different culture of standing in line, one where higher prices or allegedly higher quality products does not guarantee shorter queues. In contexts such as these we attribute to our fellow human beings a minimal degree of rationality and order, which is constantly threatened in everyday life. This is one of the topics most clearly analyzed in Larry David's brilliant show *Curb Your Enthusiasm*.

In Germany, one has to pay the supermarket protection money, as it were. We accordingly imagine that there is someone supposed to know how all of this works and we put our trust in this person – the supermarket manager or some other kind of ultimate supervisor. The social order is always dependent upon our assumption that there is a subject that knows and cares for this order. This subject takes on many forms: the law, the police, the state, the boss, the supermarket manager, the air-traffic controller, and even the scientist. The positing of an anonymous subject of knowledge which takes care of the order is a form of fetishism of which we can never fully divest ourselves. With Lacan, we can also refer to this as "the big other," or just "big brother."

With his thesis of the "disenchantment of the world," Weber draws our attention to the fact that we have placed science in the position of guaranteeing the rationality of the social order. However, in this way we excessively overburden it. For no scientific investigation will ever be able to free us from having to renegotiate the rules by which we live together in order, hopefully, to place them on a more rational foundation. We need constantly to change the various social orders in which we take part in order to adjust them in light of discoveries, changing value systems, etc. We can only hope that this process is governed by some actual rationality, but this specifically presupposes a form of new realism – that is, the idea that we human beings are capable of finding out what is the case about us. Our thoughts, values, minds, beliefs, hopes, pains, and fears have to be treated as realities as worthwhile as such denizens of reality as elementary particles, galaxies, gravity, and forests. The contemporary fetishizing of science contributes to a situation wherein we project our desire for order and our representations onto a council of alleged experts, who are supposed to relieve us of the burden of having to decide how we ought to live.

Fetishism

Against this background one can distinguish two forms of religion. The scientific worldview belongs to the first form of religion. The first form of religion is fetishism, that is to say, the creation of representations of an all-inclusive, all-controlling and ordering world principle. In contrast to this, the second form of religion is the expression of our sense and taste for the infinite, as the Romantic philosopher and theologian Friedrich Schleiermacher defined the concept of religion in his classic *On Religion*.[62]

Schleiermacher begins from the assumption that the object of religion is "the universe and the relationship of humanity to it,"[63] where, by "universe," he means the infinite in which we find ourselves. According to Schleiermacher, it is not only the universe that is infinite but also our orientation towards it. There is not merely one single intuition or description of the infinite, one single true religion in the sense of the notion that religions are specific systems of belief, but instead an infinite number:

> Every intuition of the infinite exists wholly for itself, is dependent upon no other, and has no other as a necessary consequence; they are infinitely many and have no reason in themselves why they should be related to one another in one way and not in some other, and yet each appears completely different if it is viewed from another point or related to another intuition; thus the whole of religion cannot possibly exist otherwise than when all these different views of each intuition that can arise in such a manner are really given. This is not possible except in an infinite multitude of different forms . . .[64]

Against a widespread prejudice according to which religion is associated with a dogmatic, one-sided worldview that is, in principle, intolerant of other alternatives, Schleiermacher understands religion on the basis of its orientation towards an inconceivable and incomprehensible infinite as "infinite in all respects, an infinity of matter and form, of being, of vision, and of knowledge about it."[65] In the second speech in *On Religion*, he goes so far as to designate religion as "atheism,"[66] because not all religions are theistic or even monotheistic: "God is not everything in religion, but one, and the universe is more."[67] At the time this was an outrageous statement, which was passed by the Prussian department of censorship only by accident (the censor was sick). Even though Schleiermacher is not generally recommending atheism, he still brings up the point that the meaning of religion in general should not be reduced to particular religions,

such as the Judeo-Christian-Islamic tradition of mono-
theism, because Hinduism and Buddhism are equally
important. Schleiermacher develops the meaning of
religion from a perspective of maximum openness. For
it is exactly this approach – namely, that other people
can also have justified beliefs about the infinite (because
of its/his/her complexity and transcendence with respect
to our human finitude) – that underlies a religious principle of tolerance according to which there are other
standpoints that are valuable in themselves and ought to
be protected. Tolerance in this minimal sense is actually
one of the great achievements of the history of religion.

That religion is often enough accompanied by murder
and homicide is to be ascribed to the first form of
religion rather than the second. Indeed, no religion is
completely free from fetishism – even atheism. The rev-
erence of the meaningless, purely material universe also
has a religious character. Schleiermacher recognized
this. He himself expressly defined "naturalism" as "the
intuition of the universe in its elementary multiplicity,
without the idea of personal consciousness and will of
individual elements,"[68] which in the main corresponds
to the scientific worldview, which is allegedly completely
of this world. The scientific worldview, however, is just
one religion among others – yet another blind attempt
to breathe meaning into history.

Even though it is part and parcel of a broad ideology
characterizing the idea of progress in many Occidental
societies, it is absurd to believe that there actually are
states utterly free from religious constraints. Nicholas
Ray's film *Bigger than Life* can be read as a very deep
illustration of this circumstance. Somewhere in the USA,
1956: Ed Avery does not earn enough as a teacher to
take care of his family and works additional hours in
a call center. One day he collapses. As it turns out, he
has a very rare disease that affects his arteries which can
only be treated with cortisone. Overreacting to his diag-

nosis, Ed takes too much cortisone, which he cannot survive without, and it triggers a psychosis. As the psychosis worsens, it leads to a delusion of grandeur: Ed becomes "bigger than life," which is underscored by skillful camera work. He gets caught up in a religious delusion and thinks that he must sacrifice his son, like Abraham once did with Isaac. His desperate wife, in her attempt to safeguard her son from his father, points out that in the Bible God had prevented the human sacrifice. But Ed insists that God had simply been mistaken, and in fact attempts to kill his son, which his own hallucinatory state prevents him from doing just in time. When he comes around from his fit, he is still partially caught up in his delusion, and his gaze turns to a certain Dr Norton, whom he identifies as Abraham Lincoln. Ed replaces Abraham, the biblical father, with Abraham Lincoln, whom he then identifies with the doctor. Here Ray refers us to a subtext of American political culture: Abraham is the founder of religion and one of the founding fathers of the USA – who is not doing too well with his son, the American people, which one understands by the fact that the teacher is underpaid. This theme is also central to the much acclaimed TV series *Breaking Bad*, in which a brilliant but underpaid chemistry teacher, who is sick with lung cancer, produces and sells drugs in order to pay his doctor's bills and provide support for his family should he succumb to his illness.

Nicholas Ray advances the opinion that American society associates quasi-psychotic religious, scientific, and religious authorities together. Many *film noir* directors, but also famous directors such as John Huston, deal with the oppressive mechanisms of American society by creating explicit movies of the big other, of the subject who is supposed to know, and his pathologies in order to suggest a way out (Huston even directed a Freud biopic, *Freud: The Secret Passion*, based originally on a screenplay by Jean-Paul Sartre, though never realized in that form). Societies have personalities, as it were – that is, they can be regarded as systems of models of action and interpretation that give rise to psychologically difficult situations and correlative forms of sickness or pathology. It is hardly a coincidence that the existing order of society promotes depression, which is currently the most widespread form of mental illness.

Against this background, we should learn to discern a pathology in the very idea that religion is nothing but a form of superstition we can expect to eradicate in the near future. This is even less likely given the manifold crises of the Middle East. We need to face the real challenge of religion – namely, the fact that there is no such thing as a secular society, but only secular subsystems overestimating their intellectual influence on the rest of humanity because they believe they have finally found the right kind of world picture: the scientific world picture. Yet, in my view, it is exactly this attitude which creates new forms of confrontation, as it is no different from the much criticized religious intolerance. It is an erroneous belief of simple-minded critics of religion that religion is a kind of bad scientific explanation constantly invoking "God, the father" or some other kind of extraterrestrial superpower in order to account for natural phenomena. If this is our picture of religion, no wonder we cannot understand how anyone could ever be both minimally rational and religious!

If one takes into account the fetishistic character of the scientific worldview, it ceases to be surprising that it is seen in competition with religion. For, strictly speaking, it is itself another kind of religion. No wonder, in our lifetimes we have witnessed the rise of Scientology as a new form of religion. Scientology (just think here of the utopian religious character of so many Tom Cruise movies) exploits just this feature of the scientific worldview. In order to understand this, we need to take into account that religion is not just the assumption that there exists a God (or gods) who guides every-thing, whether this be the God of the Bible, the gods of Hinduism, or the physical world formula out of which all natural laws can be derived. Fetishism consists not in venerating a particular object but in the fact that an *object* is venerated at all, without allowing any inquiry into why this object is actually so desirable or central to human action or to the infinity of what there is as such. Fetishism identifies an object as the origin of everything and attempts to develop a model of identity out of that object to which all people ought to adhere. For this reason, it is only a surface feature of a religion whether what is being venerated is a god or the Big Bang. The actual problem is the veneration of a putative universal origin – completely irrespective of what concrete object we believe to be representing this.

It is remarkable that religion often arises in connection with something of a global error theory suggesting that most of our ordinary beliefs are somehow profoundly misguided (or sinful). Typically, theories of salvation claim that the whole of reality that appears to us, the colorful world around us, in which we live and strive, is fundamentally an illusion. Thus, the aim is to know the truth behind the veil of illusion. This same gesture is characteristic of the scientific worldview. Colors, smells, sounds, and tastes are supposed to be illusions (created by our brains) behind which the true essence of things is hidden. Only the priest or the scientific expert has access to this essence. Before the Reformation he spoke in Latin; today he speaks in mathematics. Accordingly, we need another reformation, one which forces "the experts" to lay their cards on the table. It is one thing to work out a specific formal system which allows one to describe natural or social events in a language intel-ligible only to experts and another thing altogether to speak the truth. But we must not forget that "what-ever can be said can be said clearly" (to quote Ludwig

Wittgenstein again), which I interpret as meaning that every expert is an expert to the extent to which he can also communicate to the layman.

Even though Nietzsche does not use the exact word "fetishism," in a very amusing section of his book *Thus Spoke Zarathustra* he introduces the "backworldsmen," who fabricate worlds hidden beneath or beyond the surface of our ordinary views in order to distract themselves from their own situation as suffering, mortal beings.

> Intoxicating joy is it for the sufferer to look away from his suffering and forget himself. Intoxicating joy and self-forgetting, did the world once seem to me . . . Thus, once on a time, did I also cast my fancy beyond man, like all backworldsmen. Beyond man, forsooth? Ah, ye brethren, that God whom I created was human work and human madness, like all the Gods! A man was he, and only a poor fragment of a man and ego. Out of mine own ashes and glow it came unto me, that phantom. And verily, it came not unto me from the beyond![69]

Unfortunately, here Nietzsche goes a step too far, as he assumes that the human being sees only the human world. He has been taken in by constructivism.

Nonetheless, he is quite right regarding his critique of metaphysics in its manifold disguises, from Buddhism to the scientific worldview. The introduction of an "other world" is usually accompanied by an alleged insight into the structure of this other world, whether this be the claim that the world is a dream created and sustained by God himself or the claim that the world in which we live is really only a complex manifestation of elementary particles which obey natural laws and have more or less accidentally created a being who is right now typing these lines.

Fetishism is bad religion. Before Nietzsche, Marx had already pointed this out in his critique of commodity fetishism. Indeed, Marx argues that the modern division of labor is prone to fetishism because we are constantly exchanging and buying goods without knowing how they are actually produced and how their value is maintained. Marx himself draws a comparison between the socio-historical phenomenon of commodity fetishism and fetishist religion:

> In order, therefore, to find an analogy, we must have recourse to the mist-enveloped regions of the religious world. In that world the productions of the human brain appear as independent beings endowed with life, and entering into relations both with one another and the human race. So it is in the world of commodities with the products of men's hands. This I call the Fetishism which attaches itself to the products of labour, so soon as they are produced as commodities, and which is therefore inseparable from the production of commodities.[70]

A good example of the structure of fetishism is meat consumption in many contemporary societies. Let us take the very German example of a pork sausage: at first glance, pork sausage is the epitome of meat. In my neck of the woods, there even is a sausage literally called "meat sausage" [*Fleischwurst*]. Pork sausage is really a matter of chopped, seasoned, and processed meat of questionable origin and quality. Paradoxically, it is presented as if it were not really of animal origin. It is artificially formed and pressed, and usually wrapped in some form of artificial skin. When consuming meat (say, as a modern tourist visiting Berlin and loving "Currywurst," curry sausage), one typically wastes no thought at all on the animals from which it was produced. Pork sausage gives the impression that it never had anything to do with animals or animal remains. The same applies to finely packaged chicken breast or bratwurst consumed in an amusement park. This form of meat consumption is therefore fetishistic in the precise meaning of the word: pork sausage creates the impression that it came to exist all by itself in the fridge – when, in truth, at some point quite an impressive herd of pigs was rounded up, systematically slaughtered, ripped up into various pieces, and made into sausages – at best, according to health codes governing food production and, at worst, just according to local customs inherited from earlier traditions of producing sausages and the like. Thus, finding out the truth about the sausage world can be profoundly traumatic, which Christoph Schlingensief formulates in an aesthetically explosive way in his film *The German Chainsaw Massacre*. Schlingensief's film is an intense engagement with nihilism: "in a time when everything is sausage, it does not matter whether something is good or bad."*

The Infinite

However, religion is not generally blatantly fetishistic. On the contrary, in all historically created pre-modern world religions there is an opposing tendency that wants to free us from the assumption that religion boils down to the veneration of an object that is worthy of worship. In the Judeo-Christian-Islamic tradition, for example, the first commandment says that we should not make an image of God. What I have here described as "fetishism," following Marx, Nietzsche, and psychoanalysis, is in the Judeo-Christian-Islamic tradition called *idolatry*. The word comes from the ancient Greek *eidolon* (= "little picture" or "small statue of God") and *latreia* ("servile veneration"). The commandment against making an image of God represents a turn away from fetishism. It tells us to avoid the assumption that

---

* The idiomatic phrase "das ist mir Wurst" means "it's all the same to me." Likewise "alles ist Wurst" connotes a universal indifference.

we should create an image of a super-object that is worthy of our veneration, while concealing itself behind the appearances. This is a first step towards the insight that no such object exists, as I claim in this book.

I have already mentioned the formulation of Schleiermacher's above where he writes that religion is an expression of our sense and taste for the infinite. Religion in the non-fetishistic sense – that is, good religion – understands the notion of "God" as the idea of a potentially inconceivable infinite, an infinite in which we are nevertheless not lost. In this context, then, GOD is the idea that there is an infinite whole which is profoundly meaningful and also transcends our capacity to grasp it in a single unified vision. And, indeed, commitment to a belief in "God" is associated with the expression of people's confidence that there is a broader meaning to it all that both eludes us and at the same time embraces us. Religion in the non-fetishistic sense is the impression that we partake in some meaning, although it goes far beyond everything that we can fully understand. Phrases such as "the ways of the Lord are mysterious" express just this view. Just consider the following passage from the New Testament: "O the depth of the riches both of the wisdom and knowledge of God! How unsearchable are his judgments, and his ways past finding out!"[71] The author of these lines, (St) Paul, does not develop here a theory of the mathematical infinite. The depth of the wisdom and knowledge are not mathematizable or rational in our modern sense of the term. The passage also does not simply allude to the incomprehensible capriciousness of some God to whom we ought to humble ourselves. Rather, it suggests that we search for clues of meaning in what there is. Religion in the non-fetishistic sense is a search for meaning in the infinite. It assumes that there is some meaning or other of which we are a part. This is certainly true to the extent to which we not only lead our lives as arrangements of elementary particles in the universe but also appear in manifold fields of sense that cannot be described in the language of physics. There is no physics of literature or history, of revolutions or artworks, even though these fields intersect in numerous ways with fields containing elements and events open to natural scientific investigation. Trivially, what there is contains some meaning, which is not to say that the universe somehow contains a deeper meaning beneath the surface impression of a somewhat dangerous place that has certainly not been created as a habitat for *Homo sapiens* or any other life form. This idea is just absurd, and there is no necessity to interpret the book of Genesis as claiming anything like that. We also need to reject the idea that contemporary fundamentalist creationism of any sort results from taking the Bible "literally," as there is no such thing as the literal meaning of the book of Genesis which is supposed to consist in a story about how the universe came about. That this is the literal meaning of the text is already a largely unjustified assumption, an anachronistic projection of modern creationism onto ancient texts.

In other words: what is rightly attacked and rejected today as the religious worldview really has nothing to do with good religion. Religion need not be seen as a set of pseudo-scientific knowledge claims in competition with scientific theories. It does not arise from the need for an explanation of the world in the modern understanding of this word. The modern need for an explanation of worldly phenomena presupposes a conception of the world as the universe to be studied by the natural sciences. Yet, it is precisely this conception that is absent in pre-modern religious texts. Be that as it may, both the scientific and the religious worldview are false to the extent to which they are precisely what they are: namely worldviews.

Let us place ourselves at the beginning of the history of culture. Of course we do not actually know where and when this occurred or what happened. The actual history of humanity has scarcely been sufficiently studied and, what is worse, it is currently being pursued under the one-sided auspices of evolutionary theory. We actually know terrifyingly little about the history of humanity, which began *after* the somewhat successful evolutionary process of natural selection. It is misguided to think of history as the continuation of biological evolution by other means (say, culture). History is just not a biological category.

Unfortunately the conquistadors destroyed most of the artifacts of the high culture of Mesoamerica, and on the other hand there has been far too little research into the history of India to make accessible the history of that country's culture and religion. There is a great lack of knowledge of our own history even in Europe. No one really knows what happened in the so-called dark centuries of the ancient world between the twelfth and eighth centuries before Christ, when the Minoan high culture thrived on Crete. We do not even know with any degree of certainty how scientific, religious, or philosophical ideas were spread in the Mediterranean area, so that it is not clear, for example, what role the Egyptians played in the constitution of what is nowadays perceived as "the European heritage." Famously and controversially, Martin Bernal, in his three-volume work *Black Athena: The Afroasiatic Roots of Classical Civilization*, has pointed out the manifold interactions between "Western," "Occidental" or "European" civilization and Africa and Asia. Bernal is certainly right that there was no such thing as, say, "Greek" or even "European" culture that developed independently of economic, religious, and broadly intellectual interactions with Asia and Africa. As a matter of fact, the very idea of a Greek philosophy is an odd classification, as it suggests that the intellectual activity named "philosophy" by people writing and thinking in one of the dialects of ancient Greek is somehow local or national. Yet there was no such thing as "Greece" at the time when the term and maybe the practice of philosophy were invented. The so-called Presocratics spread out from what is nowadays Turkey to what is nowadays Italy (most notably southern Italy and Sicily).

Given that we will actually never really know under what conditions history began, I would like to relate my own myth in order to illustrate what might have happened. In my little story, a group of people in the dim and distant past awoke from the slumber of their merely biological existence, defined by their struggle for survival, and wondered what all of this actually meant. "Why," they asked, "do we actually hunt these animals?" "Why are we the way that we are?" Because any answer to this question (including a biological story of what it means to be a biological species) went way beyond their horizon of knowledge, the history of the first human beings began with an irritation. They just figured out that they had no idea who or what they were and started distinguishing themselves from the other animals (which may be one of the functions of their magnificent cave paintings). They were confronted with so many things which they could not understand and which were beyond their control. It was at this moment that the search for clues began. Is there an order in all that happens, maybe even a meaningful history? Religions set about telling stories and recognizing an order in the events, which incorporated people but at the same time transcended them. Religion, one might say, originally gave voice to the most radical human sense of distance, the sense that we find ourselves in a very wide context that includes us and is very hard to read.

The human being is the being that wants to know what or who it is. This situation is indeed irritating, but at least it triggered the spiritual and intellectual history of humanity, and it is simply not the case that we have found a definite answer. Remarkably, the term *"Homo sapiens"* was coined by Carl Linnaeus, who defined the human being with explicit reference (in Latin) to the imperative "Know thyself!" (*nosce te ipsum*). The history of humanity cannot be reduced to the fact that we have culture. We partake in a shared dimension of questions ("What does it all mean?" "What or who are we?"), a dimension in which we are confronted with meaning for the sake of meaning, meaning which is undecided and open.

Many philosophers have insisted that human freedom consists above all in the fact that we are not defined by any one determinate way of being, that for us there is a plurality of possible ways of being, precisely because we have no idea what our nature or essence is. Thus, even if we have a nature or essence, we will lead our lives in light of a search for meaning. This is why we can at best endorse the somewhat paradoxical notion that we do not know what our nature is, so that we constantly have to create images or ideals that help us to compensate for this profound ignorance. This is a source not only of insecurity but also of progress. However, one cannot rely on progress to realize itself. Rather, the point of human freedom lies in our capacity to move forwards and backwards: the self-determination of our very essence can fail or succeed.

The human being does not know what or who he is. We begin with the search. Being human means to be seeking for what it means to be human. Heidegger formulated this in a concise way: "Being a self is the finding that already lies *in* the seeking."[72] In order for us to search for ourselves, we must have lost a prior grasp on ourselves. There must be a distance built into our being, a distance which ultimately makes us who we are. The first experience of this distance, the experience of maximal distance, is experienced as "God" or "the divine." For this reason, the human being begins to investigate himself in the form of the divine, without recognizing that the divine that he is searching for outside himself is human spirit itself.

This means that the human being is not a ready-made hypothesis tinkerer, as the modern self-description of citizens as rational, proto-scientific subjects suggests. Humanity did not invent God, because physics had not yet occurred to us. This is also why modernity is the result of processes which we cannot understand by projecting modernity onto pre-history. Such an anachronistic and highly unscientific project is quite prevalent today. The concept of religion has been assimilated to the concept of superstition, by which one understands the belief in a demonstrably false or simply foolish hypothesis, such as the hypothesis that the movement of the heavenly bodies determines our personal life. Obviously astrology in this sense is mere superstition; however, different stages of spiritual history are here wildly mixed up. But if one understands the meaning of religion, and wants to develop a rational concept of religion, one must approach the subject in a different way.

Religion and the Search for Meaning

To this end, we must clarify a matter that appears very difficult to make sense of. This matter concerns us: our human self-consciousness. What is self-consciousness, and how does it relate to human spirit or to our mind? Today it is quite common to understand consciousness as a particular brain state with a specific function. On this model, the idea is typically that consciousness is the domain of transparent cognitive and emotional states. Consciousness comprises states that I am aware of. Yet I am, of course, not only aware of myself or my own mental states. I have a field of vision in which I am right now viewing a few things attentively; other things, in contrast, I notice only out of the corner of my eye. I feel a bit tired right now, but otherwise I generally feel well. These states are transparent to me. If this is consciousness, then we apparently already know what self-consciousness is. Self-consciousness would be the consciousness of consciousness, attentiveness to one's own consciousness, one's own processes of thought and perception. There are many important distinctions to be drawn here, distinctions philosophers have introduced in order to account for the difference between seeing a cat over there and my self-awareness of my feelings. For instance, one can distinguish *intentional* from *phenomenal consciousness*. Intentionality simply means that consciousness relates to something, that it has an object. Yet it is not clear if my own mood right now is an object of consciousness in the same way in which the cat over there is. Isn't it, rather, something that I am instead of something I relate to?

Subtleties aside, if we start from the assumption that consciousness is a kind of awareness taking place in my brain (in some of its regions, but not everywhere), it is very tempting to believe that we are sitting in our own theatre of consciousness and are watching our own reality show. Of course this show is extremely interactive, for we ourselves show up in it. In any event, consciousness would be a state, a set of states, events or processes taking place within our skull. Once again we would fall victim to neuroconstructivism, the idea that our brain constructs mental images that we are conscious of. But what else could consciousness or self-consciousness be if not something that goes on within our skull?

When I am aware, I am aware of something. This means that consciousness is always realized in relation to some object. This is called "intentionality," the stretching out of consciousness to objects. Insofar as I just distinguished my consciousness (intentionality) from all other objects and thereby achieved self-consciousness, I established a fallible relation to my consciousness as another object of consciousness. This is why I can indeed be mistaken about this object. We can certainly be wrong about what consciousness actually is, which is why it is not a matter of self-evidence. As the philosopher Daniel Dennett has emphasized time and again, the fact that we are conscious does not make us experts about consciousness.

We need to keep in mind that that of which I am aware is often not consciousness itself but, say, the sky or my fingers that are typing these lines. We are also aware of other people's consciousness. When talking to someone, I am aware that this person is either following my words or is not listening. In this sense, I am aware of another person's awareness. I can therefore quite easily be aware of the fact that someone else is aware of the fact that he is in pain. Occasionally we are also aware of the fact that we are aware. In these moments we achieve self-consciousness, which does not mean that we have achieved self-knowledge.

There is an age-old and still widely held but erroneous opinion that self-consciousness, the consciousness of consciousness, is immune from error. One might think that everyone has infallible access to themselves and knows themselves perfectly, as it were. But this is to confuse self-consciousness and self-knowledge. It might be correct to say that my consciousness of my own consciousness does indeed give me access to the fact that I am really conscious. But this does not guarantee at all that I therefore know what consciousness is, or even that I know exactly what I am aware of right now. There is no infallible form of self-knowledge, which is why there are debates about the nature of consciousness.

Because we can be deceived about what consciousness is, and because we cannot easily specify what self-consciousness actually is, we find ourselves at a distance from ourselves even on this apparently most intimate level of our very own self-awareness. We must get to know ourselves in just the same way that we get to know other objects. What is more, we change in this process of self-knowledge. Every human life has a story, which we are constantly working on, which we are constantly rewriting.

This does not apply only to the individual. The individual is known by others, and very commonly we know others better than we know ourselves. For this reason we get to know ourselves in interpersonal relationships of various kinds, such as erotic relationships or friendships. Self-knowledge is not a matter of introspection or subjectivity.

But not even consciousness and, consequently, self-consciousness can be restricted to events taking place within our skull. Let us take a look at a very simple example. Suppose that right now I am looking out of a window and believe I am perceiving a light drizzle outside. I thereby achieve self-consciousness and think to myself that I am aware of a light drizzle outside. I am conscious of my consciousness of a light drizzle outside. Now my roommate enters my study and suggests that we should clean the windows again very soon, because the dirty traces on the windowpanes create the impression that there is a light drizzle outside. My roommate can see from my reaction that I falsely believe I am aware of a light drizzle outside. It turns out that my consciousness was not, after all, consciousness of a light drizzle outside but, rather, consciousness of dirty traces on the windowpanes. The actual object of consciousness is as essential for what consciousness is as the necessary neuro-biological events taking place within my skull. This also applies to self-consciousness. It is essential for self-consciousness to be consciousness of consciousness. This means that the fact that consciousness is often about objects perceived in the environment of our bodies (the so-called external world) makes it impossible to reduce either consciousness or self-consciousness to events taking place within our skull. Philosophers like to put it this way: consciousness is not just in our heads – or, to borrow the title of a book by Alva Noë: We are "out of our heads."[73]

While we entertain further thoughts about self-consciousness, we may consult books and encyclopedia entries, have life experiences, and speculate about the concept of consciousness in order to discover what self-consciousness is all about. And this very activity is itself an exercise of what the German tradition of philosophy calls "Geist" – spirit, the self-engagement of meaning. "Geist," or spirit, differs slightly from "mind," in that it does not involve the potential confusion of a subjective realm of ideas with which we engage within our skull. We understand meaning, which is there only in order to be understood: theories, encyclopedia entries, and life experiences. In this process we assume that meaning is already there, that meaning exists which can be understood. We find meaning among the rest of what there is. This is the sense in which there is an objective spirit. There is no need to restrict the domain of what there is to everything that does not have the form of meaning. This is only a temptation for a specific version of the natural scientific worldview.

All of this means that we should fight the alienation from ourselves that describes us as biological machines to whom an I-illusion is attached, in order that the bio-mass each of us represents can reproduce and maintain an essential part of itself (our DNA or whatever it is one takes to be essential here). Anyone who understands themselves as a biological or meat machine and thinks that consciousness is actually an illusion hovering over the brain has already jumped off the cliff. It is peculiar to the human spirit that in certain individuals it can also attempt to annihilate itself (to turn itself off, so to speak), even if in many cases this does not stop the very same individual from writing weighty tomes aimed at influencing objective spirit.

Religion arises from the need to understand how the world can have meaning, how the world can be made sense of. Viewed in this way, it is quite correct to say that religion is a form of the search for meaning. As a matter of fact, religion is associated with a world picture. Yet, in contrast to the natural scientific world picture, it leaves room for the simple idea that there really is meaning, that we are not aliens in an otherwise merely physical domain who need somehow to deal with our special status by denying, eliminating or recognizing it. We are just not that special. This is literally one of the lessons one can draw from religion.

Religion arises out of the need to return to ourselves from a great distance. The human being is able to deflate its sense of self in such a way that it can understand itself as a vanishing point in an infinite expanse. Looking at ourselves from this imagined distance, we wonder whether our life actually has any meaning, or whether our hopes for meaning dissipate like drops of water in the ocean of the infinite. RELIGION is a return to ourselves from the infinite with the goal of not losing ourselves completely. It is the expression of an irritation which stirs us to take a detour around the whole because we want to understand ourselves. It derives from the impression that this movement, from ourselves to the whole and finally back again to ourselves, is not without meaning, that it is in some way of significance for the whole itself.

In this connection one can draw on the first radical philosopher of existence, the Danish philosopher Søren Kierkegaard. The philosophy of existence, which is often identified with existentialism, is a movement which does not just engage in ontology and reflect on the meaning of existence. EXISTENTIALISM is the investigation into human existence, which thinkers such as Kierkegaard,

Nietzsche, Heidegger, Sartre, or Karl Jaspers consider to be our real problem. In his work *The Sickness unto Death*, Kierkegaard differentiates between three forms of a specifically human disease which he calls "despair." He takes this sickness to be the prevailing condition of human existence, which has often been seen as too pessimistic a description. However, existentialism has recognized something important. Let us take a look at Kierkegaard's diagnosis. The three forms of despair are:

1 in Despair at Not Being Conscious of Having a Self (Despair Improperly So Called);
2 in Despair at Not Willing to Be Oneself;
3 in Despair at Willing to Be Oneself.

One can easily spell out the underlying idea. We can ask ourselves who we actually are. The history of humanity begins with this question. Human beings are distinguished from other animals insofar as we do not just follow the paths of what or who we are but change our way of looking at ourselves and of acting in light of our search for the meaning of it all. For this reason we are always discussing with one another who we *want* to be or who we actually *ought* to be. We know that we can change our own being and that we should change it in light of moral values we rightly deem central. We all know that murder and homicide should be surmounted, that world hunger should be abolished and that all people should be able to lead a prosperous life. We also know that we are at a loss in many matters. Other animals do not make much noise about their own existence in this sense, but are simply what they are. They are simply plugged into their own survival program and do not consider the thought that they should change their life. They just live it, which does not mean that they do not have consciousness or that they are biological machines. They just do not have spirit in Kierkegaard's sense, although I take it as almost self-evident that they have a conscious inner life.

Humans are differentiated from other animals neither because they think nor because they are rational. Even animals think and abide by a particular order of concepts. My dog knows where to find her food bowl and attempts to convince me to give her more food. In this interaction many concepts are in play for the dog, even if she may never know that she has concepts. To have consciousness does not presuppose that one has a theory of what consciousness is; to have concepts does not entail that one knows about having concepts. Presumably dogs do not reflect upon thinking itself, as this is a questionable privilege of human beings on our planet. Still, even this capacity to reflect on thinking is not identical to spirit. For our relationship to ourselves surely does not consist in our capacity to think about our thoughts. In principle we leave this to philosophy. Spirit is more than just reflection.

Spirit is the condition that we relate to ourselves as though we were another person, a person with whom we become acquainted and whom we sometimes want to change. We are not merely the subjects of thinking but, above all, persons, and persons relate to themselves in a context shared by other persons. In our complex self-relationship we encounter our own flexibility, which is why human existence is such a shaky affair.

The human being can suffer from insecurity and anxieties but is also just as capable of self-certainty or arrogance. The spectrum of the human psyche is therefore much wider than our emotions. Deep insecurity and strong confidence are not simply emotions such as scorn or joy, but expressions of spirit. Spirit can become sick; there are spiritual diseases, which are not just emotional disturbances. Thus, many diseases of the spirit are treated by having the patient first recognize the way in which her unconscious opinion of herself is leading to suffering, so that she is able to build a new relationship to herself which can henceforth be emotionally satisfying.

Spirit, writes Kierkegaard, relates itself to itself. And the way we observe ourselves, the way we see ourselves, displays our spirit. Our existence is a way of relating to ourselves, a relation that we are not always aware of. Spirit is the establishment and maintenance of our self-relation. In this way the relations we have to ourselves are always in some way the relations that we have with others. On some level, we are strangers to ourselves.

Thus, ever since the great achievements of psychoanalysis in the last century, every psychologist knows that our attitude to other people is always co-determined by our self-relation and vice versa. We behave towards others as we behave towards ourselves; we realize our own ideal of selfhood as well as our anxieties in our life with others in our manifold personal relationships. We do not just idealize our fellow human beings, we also degrade them or assume that they have properties that they do not have, because we often project onto them our own unconscious selves. This, by the way, can never be fully overcome. This is one of the reasons why we can learn from others who we are, because many traits of our own personalities are reflected back to us in an estranged way in our attitude towards others. What Sigmund Freud has called transference – that is, the redirection of the addressee of an emotional attitude – is characteristic of our relation with others. We redirect our own overall attitude towards ourselves to others. Of course, Freud believed that this is the result of our early childhood internalization of our parents' values, which is another story. But the idea remains valid that we often, as it were, deal with ourselves while we seem to be dealing with others. This is not a problem per se, as it underlies all our relations with others and cannot be overcome. There is no completely objective or impartial social interaction – unless one deals with some kind of holy or divine personality who is typically described as leaving their family and home in order to join humanity as such (just think of Jesus or Buddha here). But then there is the paradox that leaving one's family and joining humanity does not make one logically less incomplete, as one now becomes a devotee of humanity and creates special alliances against the other animals or, at the very least, against those who do not wish to leave their limited and local relations in order to join the party of universal humanity.

Kierkegaard does not yet have access to the major psychoanalytic concepts of the subconscious, projection and transference, but he comes close to these concepts in his analysis of the first form of despair: the self is capable of overlooking itself; it can relate to itself as if it were not there. As soon as it discovers itself, it can either attempt to hold on to itself and interrupt its earlier unconscious dynamics, or it can attempt to break free from itself and continue to work on itself by trying to become another self. Every one of us is acquainted with personalities suffering from one of these three forms of the sickness unto death, and we recognize these aspects of selfhood in ourselves. Sometimes we simply attempt to ignore ourselves, just to get rid of the difficulties of being someone at all, to become universal or neutral. At other times we try to determine ourselves in a fixed way or to change ourselves so radically that we might be someone else after the change.

For our purposes, what is decisive in Kierkegaard's analysis is the discovery that we, as spirits, relate to ourselves in such a way that we understand that it is always possible for us to change ourselves. We could indeed become someone different; we look at ourselves and the realities with which we are confronted in a different light. This is why we constantly compare ourselves with other people in one way or another and reflect on which form of life is most suitable for us. It is exactly at this point that Kierkegaard's God comes into play. For he defines "God" as the fact "that everything is possible."[74] By this he means that we encounter God or the divine if we grasp the very idea of a maximal distance from ourselves and find that everything – most notably, a different attitude towards others and ourselves – is possible. This is shown existentially in our lives when we lose the earth from beneath our feet and understand that we could take up completely different lifestyles, because we are capable of adopting different attitudes towards ourselves. We realize a few of these in our lives, others not. No one is simply a self in the way that a stone remains a stone. Yet at every stage of our lives we re-create the impression that we have achieved a stable self on the basis of some kind of insight into who we ought to be, and we tend to forget who we once were in order to treat our present self as more important than our past and our future selves, often to the detriment of the latter.

The Function of God

I do not mean to claim that God really exists – in the sense that there is a person who imposes laws or is located in some inaccessible place outside of the universe, from which he sometimes comes down to earth in order to perform miracles. Granting meaning to religion does not simply involve a commitment to God's existence in this sense. In any event, it is obvious that God exists; the pressing question concerns in what field of sense he exists, how "God" appears. And there is really no good reason to interpret the great religious pre-modern texts as committing to God's existence in or outside the universe, in or beyond nature, as the relevant expressions "the universe" or "nature" acquired their present meaning only in modernity. In the book of Genesis, for example, "heaven and earth" does not mean "everything above our atmosphere and planet earth," as no one had any idea at that time that there was an atmosphere or that the earth was a planet. "Heaven and earth" is shorthand for "everything," a combination of words one can find from ancient Chinese texts, via the big Middle Eastern civilizations, to Greek mythology. The creation of everything is not understood as a causal process in which God uses his mental superpowers in order miraculously to bring matter into existence. This is completely anachronistic and does not respect the historical context of the texts, which must always be taken into account when we try to understand them.

The same holds for Kierkegaard's claim that "God" means that everything is possible. According to his analysis, God corresponds to our capacity to achieve a maximal distance from ourselves. This allows him to translate the major concepts of Christianity, which as a Christian theologian he understood well, into his theory of what it is to be a self, into his theory of spirit. For example, he understands "sin" as the rejection of spirit. Sin, then, is not "evil action" or "gloomy thinking" but an orientation to oneself in which one attempts to eliminate one's own spirit.

It is obvious that analogous analyses and meaningful interpretations may be carried out for other religions as well. There is not just one culturally and historically invariable meaning of religion. Needless to say, in every religion there is not just good religion (in the sense of the idea that we are involved in overall meaningful transactions) but always elements of fetishism and, accordingly, of superstition. All I am saying is that we should not identify the meaning of religion with a set of superstitious beliefs, as this will make us blind to the very need articulated in religion to the present day. And we must not forget that, in absolute numbers of believers, there has never been a more religious age than ours!

Our primary encounter with meaning is within the human realm. At some point spirit began to question itself, and it was at this moment that the history of spirit began, which has triggered the historical developments and achievements to which modern science belongs. Science, enlightenment, and religion are more similar than one might think. Just consider a major modern country such as India. Indian society is obviously very deeply affected by various religious movements, from Islam, Hinduism and Buddhism to many other smaller or larger groups, which does not prevent the country from being a modern democracy and from contributing to science and enlightenment. Presumably many more people on this planet are religious in one way or another than are completely atheistic or "religiously unmusical," as Max Weber said about himself.[75] That our social reality is very far from being free from religion cannot be explained by the assumption that religion is a completely different domain of human experience than science.

One way of looking at the objectivity of modern science (in the sense of the natural sciences) is that it is so objective precisely because it is directed at the world without spectators. And, indeed, even the study of human genetics or the discipline of medicine deals not with spirit but with our bodies, regardless of our specific attitudes towards them. Our bodies are related to our spirit – we buy clothes, groom ourselves, and express ourselves with gestures and facial expressions. None of this is understood from the standpoint of the natural sciences, precisely because they work under the justified assumption that the universe is the field of sense not inhabited by spirit. This does not mean that spirit (in the sense of objective relationship among human beings who are trying to figure out who they are) does not exist, just that it cannot be studied from the vantage point of scientific objectivity. Our body qua object of biology is not the body of human expression, the sounding board of our personality. On the face of it nothing speaks against this. We do have bodies and they can be studied scientifically. I am not at all interested here in advocating the spiritualization of medicine. Scientific progress is a blessing which can become a threat, but luckily it is not necessarily a threat.

Kierkegaard's basic idea is that science, religion, or any other picture that we make of ourselves and our position in the whole is evidence of spirit. We express a normative self-relation in every form of description, a way we want to be. Science is practiced by scientists who aim for objectivity in their discoveries. Their discoveries are related to their self-description as neutral observers interested in finding out how nature works. This does not undermine the actual objectivity of their methods or their findings. Kierkegaard calls the insight that an indefinite number of ways of relating to oneself is possible "God." This idea tells us something important about the meaning of religion, namely that good religion resists fetishism.

We cannot know everything simply because there is no principle that holds everything together and organizes it all. The world does not exist. God cannot exist, as long as by the term "God" we understand such a principle. We do not even know who we are, but find ourselves in the search for ourselves. As Kierkegaard and Heidegger recognized, we are just those beings who find ourselves in the search for a self. Every attempt to bring this search to an end via a simple answer is a form of superstition and self-deception. This holds for a reduction of spirit both to the organization of our bodies and to religious superstition equipping us with a quasi-material soul inhabiting our bodies.

Good religion is the opposite of an explanation of the world. Some version of the insight that the world does not exist is widespread in all world religions, from the

Hindu conviction that life is a dream and Jesus' famous statement that his kingdom is not of this world, all the way to the overcoming of the world in Buddhism. One could even be a bit provocative and say that the meaning of religion is the insight that God does not exist, that God is no object or super-object which guarantees the meaning of life. If one thinks that there is a great king who guides the universe and human life, one is mistaken. For there is no world whole that could be ruled by anyone. But this does not imply that religion or discourse about God is without meaning. It is actually the other way around: the meaning of religion lies in its recognition of our finitude. Religion returns us to ourselves from a journey out into maximal distance. In this way, religion has, of course, contributed to the creation of the notion of the world as a whole of which we are a part.

Without religion there would never have been metaphysics, without metaphysics there would never have been science, and without science we would never have been able to move into modernity. Modernity should be seen not as an overcoming of religion (which it is not, as the facts tell us) but as the ideal that we should expand our understanding of freedom. In this way, in modernity the human being has come to recognize that he is spirit and that this spirit has a history. This dimension was previously hidden to us or available only in a rudimentary way. We need to rehabilitate the notion of religion as well as that of spirit in order to be able to understand what religion is. If we do not understand it, we will behave irrationally towards it, which is certainly an element in the many current historical crises. Religion is based at least implicitly on a recognition of spirit. For some it will sound paradoxical, but religion is more pluralistic than the natural scientific worldview, as it grants reality and existence to human spirit in addition to the field of sense of nature. That it often fetishizes spirit is another concern, and I do not doubt this. Obviously there are deficient forms of religion, mere superstition and manipulative sects. But in the same way there are deficient forms of science and scientific error, without which there would be no scientific progress.

The elimination of spirit is itself spirit, certainly spirit in its worst form – spirit in its self-renouncement – "Despair Improperly So Called," as Kierkegaard terms it. This is why one must approach the question concerning God's existence much more carefully than fetishistic sects or historically uninformed neo-atheists believe. The question concerning God's existence cannot be dealt with independently of our recognition of the history of spirit itself. Many thinkers in the tradition of post-Kantian German philosophy and also Hans-Georg Gadamer have correctly emphasized this. God's existence is not a problem of the natural sciences, because it is self-evident that God is not found in the universe. One may rightly dispose of every religion that assumes this, because it exhibits the form of fetishism and is accordingly erroneous by its own standards, as long as it is recognized that idolatry is prohibited by the monotheistic God accepted alike by Judaism, Christianity and Islam. It is not the case that religion as such is fetishistic. Rather, religion deals with human beings and their place in a context of meaning. We cannot "outsource" this activity by hiring experts, because, when it comes to being human, there are no experts who could take from our shoulders our responsibility to become who we are.

VI

The Meaning of Art

Why is it that we like to visit museums, concerts, the movies, or the theatre? "Entertainment" is no sufficient answer to the question. For many works of art are not very entertaining, at least not in the immediate sense of the word. What is the attraction of art? The classical answer is the idea of the beauty of works of art. But this does not work either, because many works of art are repugnant and ugly. To say that even ugly works of art are actually beautiful undermines the contrast between the beautiful and the ugly employed in the history of art itself. Why should the women depicted in Picasso's *Les Demoiselles d'Avignon* be beautiful? The point of this and many other works of art (whether a horror film or a dissonant piece of music) consists in breaking down the concept of beauty in order to undermine the thesis that art is a form of entertainment.

Let us approach the question concerning the meaning of art from another perspective. We go to the museum because we experience there the freedom to see things differently. By interacting with art we learn to free ourselves from the assumption that there is a fixed world order in which we are merely passive spectators. Passive spectators don't understand what they are encountering in a museum. One must make an effort to interpret a disturbing and apparently meaningless work of art.

184

Without interpretation, without the effort to understand the apparently unintelligible, one sees only blots of color, not just in the works of Jackson Pollock, but even in those of Michelangelo. The field of sense of art shows us straightaway that some meaning exists only where we actively engage with it. It thereby shows us that meaning exists without having to be discovered, that some things exist in fields of sense to which we belong.

The meaning of art is that it makes us confront sense.* Sense normally allows objects to appear which then stand before the sense and hide it, as it were. This is literally the case with the sense of vision. The objects that are seen appear before the sense of vision and hide the fact that they are seen. We see objects, but we do not see our seeing of the objects. The sense of vision is transparent in that it lets us see things, but not the seeing of things. However, in the visual arts we are made aware of our viewing habits, of the way in which we see objects. We are confronted with the sense itself, not just with what is sensed. This also applies to music, where we learn something about the structure of our sense of hearing. We do not just hear sounds, as in everyday life, but we experience at the same time something about hearing itself. Painting, film, and less orthodox arts such as haute cuisine, which makes an object out of our eating habits and changes our sense of taste, work similarly. Art frees us from our detachment to objects by placing us in a different orientation towards them. Art displaces the objects from the fields of sense in which they normally arise so that the way in which they appear becomes intelligible to us.

---

* The original German is "der Sinn der Kunst," which is "the sense of art." "Sense" here has been translated as "meaning," since this is what most naturally expresses the German meaning. However, this covers up the reflexivity that is obvious in the German, namely that the "sense" of art is that it makes us confront sense, and accordingly it puts us face to face with fields of sense that are normally hidden by the object.

Ambivalences

Since antiquity there has been a disagreement about whether we can learn anything from art – whether art contains truth or just illusions. The distinction between reality and fiction is associated with this debate. Today, this distinction is often drawn in such a way that it requires the existence of fictional worlds, supposedly created by virtue of people talking not about "real" objects, persons, and events but, rather, about merely "possible," "fictional," or "imagined" objects, persons, and events. A comprehensive way of spelling this out relies on the distinction between sense and reference proposed by the German mathematician and philosopher Gottlob Frege. By the sense of an expression, Frege understands the way some object or complex of objects is represented as being, while reference is his name for the object or complex of objects to which the expression refers. This implies that there can be expressions, such as proper names, which have a sense (we can understand what they mean) but do not refer to anything. This is called the assumption of empty names. In this connection, Frege himself speaks of "legends and poetry,"[76] where he considers the idea of reference-free, yet meaningful pieces of language. For him, proper names that occur in fiction, such as "Ulysses" or "Doctor Who" (if it is a proper name), do not denote real objects; they have sense but no reference.

Yet what should we say when it comes to proper names such as "Troy" or "Venice"? Many events and places in Greek mythology and literature refer to Athens, Troy, Thebes, or other cities, which were very well known to the ancient Greeks. And Thomas Mann's *Death in Venice* concerns an actual location, Venice, with which his readers are familiar and have perhaps even visited. Earlier we hinted at Proust's brilliant invention of an artist named Elstir, whose paintings –

non-existent in comparison with Picasso's – the narrator perfectly describes in *In Search of Lost Time*. On the other hand, the narrator also refers to Monet and his paintings so that, within Proust's novel, "real" as well as "fictional" works of art are discussed. The contrast between Elstir and Monet plays an important role in the novel, just as the contrast between hallucination and reality does within the narrative of *Death in Venice*. This is why understanding art generally either as a mere replication or copy of the appearing world or as fiction in contrast with reality does not work.

Literature and theatre are not the only arts which consistently undermine the supposedly clear distinction between reality and fiction in various ways. Films such as *The Matrix*, *Inception*, or many contemporary neo-noir classics are also great examples: *Fight Club*, *Memento* and *Shutter Island*, as well as most films by David Lynch and *The Truman Show*. These films transplant us into strange situations, so that we are not certain exactly what the rules are according to which the narrated world functions, in which field of sense we find ourselves. Are we currently aware or are we dreaming? Am I really the person I appear to be? How do we know that we are not completely schizophrenic and merely imagine a great part of our life? With a little fantasy one can easily recognize how many aspects of our life are in fact imaginary or completely symbolic. In social interaction, a lot hinges on how we conceive the perspectives of other people towards themselves, towards us, and towards objects that we talk about. We constantly coordinate our imaginary depiction of how we and other objects appear to others in order to locate ourselves in a common environment. Without fantasy there would be neither reality nor objects, which each of us perceives quite differently in light of our own experience. We can only inhabit the same social setting by imagining how others relate to the equivalent scene of interaction.

The American philosopher Stanley Cavell writes pith-
ily in a book about the ontology of film:

> It is a poor idea of fantasy which takes it to be a world
> apart from reality, a world clearly showing its unreality.
> Fantasy is precisely what reality can be confused with.
> It is through fantasy that our conviction of the worth
> of reality is established; to forgo fantasies would be to
> forgo our touch with the world.[77]

The meaning of art can be sought neither in the idea that
art is entertainment nor in the idea that it imitates reality and is therefore less real, merely fictional or possible.
On the contrary, it shows us a picture, a self-portrait, a
portrait of our times, a representation of taste, or a pure
representation of sound. Certainly the picture that art
communicates is always ambivalent and can be interpreted in many diverse ways (which does not mean that
the interpretations are arbitrary).

Let us now turn for an example to a painting by
Vermeer. Vermeer often paints domestic scenes, rooms
where light falls through a window, thereby exploring
both the relation between the light source and color and
the idea of subjectivity or selfhood as an internal space.

The painting *Girl Reading a Letter by an Open
Window* plays with the difference between reality and
fiction or being and appearance on many different levels.
The light shines through the window onto the scene
from an invisible light source on the left, which attracts
our attention. The setting opens itself up to us like a
stage: the curtains are drawn in the foreground in such
a way that the structure of the painting is punctuated.
It is a stage to be observed by us. The girl has received
a letter; it is presumably a love letter. Her cheeks are
colored a light red, which one might interpret as shame.
Moreover, the curtains are the same color as her dress,
which, with a little psychoanalytic wit, one might interpret such that the spectator (namely ourselves) is almost

undressing the girl with his eyes. For we observe her in an intimate scene. One can also see a further indication of the sexual undertones of the painting in the fruit bowl that has been tipped over, out of which a half-eaten peach has tumbled; moreover, the bowl is located on an unmade bed.

It is conspicuous that the girl is not turned towards the light but instead is reflected in the windowpane while she anxiously reads the letter. One might interpret this as a critical allusion to the motif of sin: the girl turns away from the godly light and towards earthly appetites. On this reading, our position as the viewer becomes questionable, because we find ourselves in the role of a peeping tom. We are just like the girl reading the letter, for in our act of interpreting the painting we turn from the godly light and take up an earthly point of view. The spectator might be attracted by the idea that the girl receiving the letter is erotically aroused. It can be left open as to whether one would prefer to understand the painting as a call to overcome earthly desires or, much better, as a straightforward ironic critique of this idea. At first glance, both interpretations are possible.

One thing which is generally important when it comes to Renaissance painting is of course the relationship between light and color, which is explored in such a way that ordinary scenes – such as that of a girl reading a letter by an open window – appear glorified and more sublime. Color, which was despised and denounced during the modern scientific revolution as an illusion created by our senses, becomes the very medium through which the meaning of art is articulated. It is no coincidence that art discovers light in its relation to color and human meaning at the same time as color is reduced to a kind of illusion in the early modern scientific revolution. Art thereby asserts its ontological dignity, the fact that it constitutes a field of sense that exists with the same right as nature studied by the natural sciences.

On Sense and Reference

The meaning of art lies in its ability to acquaint us with the ambivalence of sense. Art shows that objects only ever appear in fields of sense, insofar as art brings its objects to appearance by connecting them with the sense in which they appear. This thesis requires elucidation, for which we must take a small theoretical detour.

In the first chapter we saw that there are various domains of objects – for example, the domain of physics and the domain of art history. But how do we actually differentiate the domains of objects? What makes an object domain what it is and distinguishes it from others? Or, as philosophers like to put it, what are the criteria for the individuation of object domains?

In "Sense and Reference," Gottlob Frege understands the sense of an expression as a "mode of presentation" of the object it is supposed to refer to.[78] He emphasized that the way an object is presented has nothing to do with our subjectivity. Modes of presentation are as objective as it gets. Let us use a simple example to illustrate the point. That Vesuvius appears differently when viewed from Sorrento than it does from Naples does not lie in the eye of the beholder but is a fact. The mode of presentation of Vesuvius as seen from Sorrento has nothing to do with our associations or representations, which we may or may not connect with the expression "Vesuvius as seen from Sorrento." Maybe one thinks about the color blue whenever one hears the word "meerkat." Yet this has nothing to do with the sense of the expression "meerkat." The expression "meerkat" has a sense, and this sense equips us with the means to identify meerkats when confronted with them. By the "reference" of an expression, Frege understands the object to which the expression refers. The idea behind the term "fields of sense" is that object domains are individuated by being defined by senses. The object domain of Spanish citizenship, for example, is individuated by the way we come to present someone as a Spanish citizen. Also, object domains that are not produced or co-produced by our beliefs about them – such as the domain of moons in our solar system – are not free from sense. The fact that the moon looks the way it does from here is not external to what the moon is. The moon itself looks the way it does from here. That the moon looks the way it does from here under our specific optical conditions is a fact involving the moon itself and not just our representation of it. Senses are, in other words, the ways things are in themselves.

To return to our first example, if one does not take this into account, it would appear as though there were, on the one hand, a volcano, Vesuvius, which, on the other hand, contingently looks a certain way from Sorrento and another way from Naples. However, one cannot oppose sense and reference, fields of sense and the objects and facts that appear in them, in this way. This would throw us back to old realism or metaphysics, in that we would return to the idea of a single homogeneous domain of objects (reality, the all-encompassing world), to which we have access by virtue of various modes of presentation (our perspectives). But this set-up again ignores the fact that our perspectives are part of reality, however we want to think about an all-encompassing reality. In any event, we cannot look at reality from the outside, as no such outside is available. This is why it is profoundly incoherent to oppose reality and appearance by assuming that there is an aperspectival reality to which we direct our potentially distorting registries in order to create perspectives onto things from nothing.

Sense itself exists; it belongs to the objects just as much as the condition that objects belong to a domain of objects. It is not external to the objects or the domain to which they belong. Whether my desk belongs to the field of sense "imagination" or the field of sense of my office is a difference that makes a difference.

However, in order to appreciate the meaning of art, we must take a step beyond our knowledge that objective senses exist. Here we can once again follow a hint from Frege. For besides sense he introduces another category, which he describes as "coloring" or "shading."[79] This category is effective, for example, in the difference between "dog" and "cur," which is not a difference of sense but a difference of shading. We see a dog in a different light when we treat it as a cur rather than as a dog.

All objects appear in specific ways; they are presented to us in different ways. Everything always appears in a certain kind of light. Because objects can be presented in many different ways they can belong to many different fields of sense. What I mean by "sense" also always includes the "shading," the "fragrance" of an expression or a thought.

At first glance one might think that works of art have so many different meanings one can hardly argue about them. Everything seems to be dependent upon the contingent impression that they make on us. In art anything goes, or so it seems. But, if this assumption were literally true, there would be no objective interpretations. A good deal of literary studies and its interpretations of texts would consist only in subjective impressions laid down by scholars in their respective fields. However, just because one can interpret poems in different ways, it does not follow that these various interpretations are not objective, at least in the minimal sense that they can be assessed as apt or inadequate, or, in other words, as correct or incorrect.

Most objects appear to us without their way of appearing also appearing to us. Right now a couple smoking cigarettes is walking past my window. I am not necessarily conscious of the way the pair appears. One can understand many objects without having the slightest idea of how one understands them. Philosophers typically think about the way in which they think about something. Philosophy is a practice in which one learns to think about thinking itself. REFLECTION is the practice of thinking about thinking. In this context, objects no longer simply appear to us, as we also become aware of the way in which they appear to us. One no longer looks directly into and observes what happens in a field of sense. Reflection is one way of accessing the framing of a scene or the conceptual framework of a theory, which does not make reflection less objective or scientific. In a way, one shifts the emphasis from the objects in a domain of objects to the individuality of the domain itself, and thus one achieves knowledge of its sense.

Now, art does indeed confront us with pure sense, which does not mean that there are no objects or no reality in it. We do not have the experience of confronting sense only in art or philosophy. A greater treasure trove of experience is traveling, by which I do not mean common tourism, which is not really traveling but, rather, a change of location in search of better weather, or in order to take pictures, or to send postcards. On a real trip one experiences a certain foreignness. How people relate to the environment of another culture may appear strange to us, perhaps even nonsensical. We must attempt to find rhyme and reason in their behavior, which means that we must search for the sense or meaning of a different field of sense in which we suddenly find ourselves. In a familiar environment, in contrast, we are mostly oriented in the field of sense and its objects – our daily rituals and routines are designed in such a way that we remain in control of objects. Ordinary objects in our everyday lives do not surprise us with unforeseen coloring or shading but instead can be processed without trouble.

The meaning of art consists in putting that which

is normally self-evident into an unconventional light: art puts an action on the stage, films it, frames it, develops a symphony with an unexpected chord at a crucial moment, or speaks the unforeseeable language of a successful poem. Art surprises us with new sense and illuminates objects from an unfamiliar perspective. Many artists have recognized and investigated this connection.

The Demon of Analogy

Let us use as an example a small prose poem by Stéphane Mallarmé entitled *The Demon of Analogy*.[80] In this poem, a voice is heard by the narrator speaking the absurd sentence "The Penultimate is dead." In Latin, the "penultimate" is the next to last syllable of a word, which plays an important role in the composition of Latin verse. The sentence seems to mean nothing at all: how can a syllable be dead? It may be taken as meaningless, which is also the first suspicion of the narrator, who complains about "the damned fragrance of a meaningless phrase."[81] At the same time, a vision befalls him:

> of a wing, gliding over the strings of an instrument, languid and light, which was replaced by a voice pronouncing these words in a falling tone: "La Penultième est morte" – such that
> > La Penultième
> *ended the verse and*
> > > est morte
> detached itself from the fateful suspension, trailing uselessly into the void of signification.[82]

The narrator cannot get the sentence out of his head; he almost staggers through the street, until suddenly he finds himself before a store that sells antique musical instruments. At this moment he repeats the sentence to himself once again, and while he is repeating it he notices that musical instruments are hanging in the window. He recognizes "on the ground, yellow palms and ancient birds, their wings shrouded in shadow."[83] The vague vision triggered by the apparently absurd sentence is thereby objectified and verified in a surprising way. The apparently absurd sentence opens up a truth for him, which his "masterful spirit"[84] until then had believed to be an absurdity.

Many insights may be culled from this prose poem. The narrator himself emphasizes that he hears the syllable "nul" in the word "penultimate," which means "null." For the narrator, the French word sounds like "Pe-*nul*-tième." He analyzes it in such a way that he encounters a form of nothingness or meaninglessness. At first he hears only the nonsense, the absurdity, the absence of meaning. This corresponds to Frege's idea that proper names in poetry are empty names. Poetry seems to boil down to a chain of representations that fail to refer to anything but which, nevertheless, are able to evoke vague representations in us through the "fragrance" of words. The narrator describes this situation with the sentence "the Penultimate is dead," which to all intents and purposes one can understand as the claim that verse poetry has come to an end. Proper compliance with the penultimate belongs to rules of emphasis of Latin, which a Latin poet must consider in order to fashion a verse. There is, therefore, a meaning we can attach to the phrase "the Penultimate is dead" – for instance, that Latin verse poetry has come to an end – which need not imply the death or end of poetry as such.

When the narrator suddenly recognizes that his vision is, as it were, confirmed by the presence of objects in the window of the antique store, the impression of absurdity, of the vacuum of meaning, is cancelled. His words turn out of the blue into something meaningful, what

is identified in the piece as "the irrefutable intervention of the supernatural."[85] The supernatural here is
Mallarmé's name for truth.[86] An apparently meaningless and senseless sentence turns out by coincidence to
be true. Thereby, the truth of the sentence exceeds the
psychological state of the subject, to whom this sentence
appears as nothing more than an involuntary incursion.
For Mallarmé, such an accident can become the very
vehicle of meaning.

In this way, his little prose poem calls our attention to
a fundamental condition of our perception and thought,
because it regularly happens that there occurs to us a
sentence which turns out to be true. When I think that
it is raining, and it is actually raining, my belief that I
can express this with a sentence turns out to be true.
We do not produce thoughts arbitrarily, as though we
were standing behind our thoughts and then attempted
to figure out what thoughts we were actually thinking
or ought to be thinking. Rather, in many situations the
thought that it is raining is "evoked or wrung" from us
by the rain – to use the terminology of the American
philosopher Wilfrid Sellars.[87] Every true and linguisti-
cally articulated thought is in the end just as surprising
as the "inexplicable penultimate."[88] We only ever connect our thoughts after the fact that we have them, and
in this way we order our current set of beliefs. This
procedure is indeed governed by various norms, some
of which are the laws of logic, which does not mean that
we are always thinking in the form of logically organized argumentation. However, this does not mean that
our representations float about meaninglessly before
us, sometimes animated by poetry and sometimes dis-
ciplined by logic. Poetry is just as capable of truth as
a well-grounded mathematical theorem. They have in
common that a thought has to occur to someone and
has to stand in an appropriate relation to what has to be
the case in order for it to be true.

An important difference between true beliefs about ordinary events such as the rain and truth in poetry lies in the fact that poetry always also speaks about itself. Poetry is not just about what is said, what is stated, but also about the act of speaking itself. In poetry language itself comes into consideration; poetry speaks about language, or, more exactly, it speaks about the successful encounter between language and reality. This is exactly what the prose poem by Mallarmé shows.

Reflexivity

In our age of naturalism the very idea of the meaning of art is hard to grasp, because it does not consist in a mapping relation between art and nature, an idea that since its inception has been heavily under attack in modern art theory. Although we all go to the movies, concerts, and museums, nowadays there is the tendency to misjudge the aesthetic experience as mere entertainment. Does it not seem as though art were merely a titillation of our neurons, a certain way of stimulating our bodies and our brains? Is art just a drug, as many contemporary TV shows such as *Breaking Bad* suggest? This way of seeing things is the consequence of an illegitimate generalization of our natural-scientific stance. It is as though we were constantly viewing ourselves through an X-ray picture that presents only a phantom of ourselves and stems from the natural sciences.

Rather than speaking about shading or the fragrance of an expression (like Frege), Sigmund Freud, in his *The Joke and its Relation to the Unconscious*, introduces the notion of a "psychological accent" and develops a theory of the laws of its displacement, which is motivated by the idea that the unconscious manifests itself through sequences of tones.[89] A famous example of Freud's concerns a patient, Mr E., who once had a panic attack when he tried to capture a black bug.[90] During the analysis it came to light that his first nanny, for whom he harbored unconscious erotic feelings, was French, which led him to the expression "Que faire?" (meaning "What on earth should I do?"). This he connected with a statement made by his aunt, according to whom his mother is said to have been undecided about her marriage. The French "que faire" sounds a bit like the German word for "bug" [Käfer]. The demon of analogy transforms "que faire" into "bug," making it possible for the repressed content to resurface (to be acted out) in the form of a bug phobia. As Freud interprets it in this context, in the German word for "bug," the repressed desire for the nanny came together with the issue of Mr E.'s relationship with his mother (his mother's name was Marie, and in German "Marienkäfer" means "ladybug") and his mother's reluctance to marry his father.

Freud's theory of jokes and their relation to the unconscious can be illustrated nicely by the comedy *Salami Aleikum* by Ali Samadi. Already the title of the film exemplifies what Freud has in mind. The Arabic salutation, to which the title of the film *Salami Aleikum* is alluding, is, of course, "salam aleikum" where "salam" means peace. It is replaced by salami, the sausage. Salami replaces peace. The title evidently proves that we can expect a comedy, precisely because the unusual association between salami and "salam" is funny. It evokes an unusual contrast and replaces a serious word (peace), which stands for a norm of adult social life, with the unconscious wish to make fun of it, to turn it into a funny object (a salami). Freud would probably add that the invocation of a salami has erotic undertones, but I leave that aside.

The contrast between salam and salami also determines the essential content of the film, as may be seen from a rough outline of the plot. The son of a butcher from Cologne with Iranian roots wants to become a butcher himself. This means that his father has to teach him to produce sausage. The necessity of slaughter in the movie is generally contrasted with the ban on killing, especially after Moshen (a German with Iranian roots from West Germany), the protagonist, falls in love with Ana (from East Germany), who is a vegetarian. In this way, peace and salami are surprisingly closely connected and opposed to each other. The ground for further oppositions in the plot – East Germany and West Germany, Germany and Persia, men and women, communism and capitalism – is prepared through the humorous contrast in the title of the film. The amusing oppositions driving the plot's development help our unconscious to be expressed in laughter and allow us to focus attention on things which would otherwise remain repressed. Our subconscious desires and fears are indirectly addressed so that we do not have to confront them as such.

Freud believes that jokes displace the psychological significance of a word in such a way that it evokes unconscious associations that we can laugh about without becoming aware of them for what they are. Jokes confront what is normally suppressed, and they indirectly make us aware of our unconscious while at the same time disguising this process, so that no direct threat to our psychological stability arises. If one digs a little deeper, one will eventually reach the unconscious, which according to Freud does not respect the customary laws of rationality or logic, most notably the norms that tell us to avoid contradictions and to strive for coherent systems of ideas and clear and articulate thoughts.

> For the infantile is the source of the unconscious. The unconscious mental processes are no others than those which are solely produced during infancy. The thought which sinks into the unconscious for the purpose of

> wit-formation only revisits there the old homestead of
> the former playing with words. The thought is put back
> for a moment into the infantile state in order to regain in
> this way childish pleasure-sources.[91]

Humor as well as art in general draws on the "pleasure which results from the freedom of thought"[92] and temporarily frees us from the compulsion to think purely rationally, a compulsion which we impose upon ourselves in light of our desire as members of social orders for self-control. It creates a distance between ourselves and objects and shows us their sense regardless of our rational expectations. In this way, art holds a mirror before us, which a critical comedy such as *Salami Aleikum* skillfully takes advantage of. The movie, among other things, deals with complex prejudices towards other forms of thought and culturally entrenched behavior, without assuming that any one of them is dominant or defines overall norms. Prejudices are congealed fields of sense which we can challenge with the help of art and humor.

Through a work of art we see not only an object but always one or many objects that appear together with their sense. Works of art are reflexive fields of sense in which objects appear not only as objects (as is the case in any field of sense) but at the same time as objects *within* a field of sense. The objects of art appear in art together with their sense – and in infinitely many varieties.

Let us compare two examples: Kasimir Malevich's famous *Black Square* and, again, Vermeer's *Girl Reading a Letter by an Open Window*. At first sight one might think that these works have nothing in common: Vermeer's painting is figurative, while Malevich's is completely abstract. Vermeer's painting is colorful, while Malevich's consists of nothing but a black surface on a white background. Abstract art seems to be abstract in that it does not contain or depict any objects.

How can one claim that abstract art is about a reflexive field of sense in which an object appears together with its sense if there are no objects in it? And in what way is Vermeer's painting actually reflexive?

Let us begin with a simple observation, namely that Malevich's painting is not really without an object. Rather, it depicts a very common object, a black square on a white background. How is this not an object? Certainly, in earlier eras one might have expected more from art, in particular a depiction of some object relevant to human beings. Black squares just don't seem to be objects befitting the content of a work of art. Malevich disappoints a certain expectation and shows in this way exactly how objects appear. For all objects appear against a background, ultimately against the background of their field of sense. Malevich's *Black Square* is not only art, it is pure art: it depicts a paradigmatic object – the black square – in a paradigmatic situation – on a white background.

That this kind of situation is paradigmatic transpires from the example of the field of vision, since it is particularly suited to representing the foreground/background metaphor. Right now I see a water bottle on my desk. It appears against the background of my desk, on which other objects are present while I look at the water bottle. However, one never catches sight of a completely unconcealed background – that is, of the background of all backgrounds. If I concentrate on the background to the water bottle (the desk), there is another background – for example, my office – which is concealed by the new foreground. There is no ultimate background, no stage setting of absolutely everything, which is another way of expressing my central tenet that the world does not exist.

Of course, I can now concentrate on my office, but then once again there will be another background to the office against which it appears. For this reason, it is really quite profound that the ancient Romans introduced the word "existence" in order to speak of what there is, as it literally means "to step forward/stand out." Everything that exists stands out against a background, which itself can never "step forward," except when it is able to transform itself into a new foreground, such as when one directs one's attention to it. But this just means that there will always be another background, be it only the background of your own thinking about something, so that this very something can appear before you as an object to be thought about.

Malevich presents exactly this interplay of background and foreground (existence) in pure form. This is why he paints a black square against a white background. We are first taken in by the object and concentrate on the black square. This creates the illusion that the work is utterly abstract – that is to say, non-representational. Then we notice that the black square stands out against a background. Now we can refer to the background too, which in turn becomes the foreground of a new background.

Malevich makes it quite clear in his theoretical writings, especially in *Suprematism – the World without Objects*, that we must go one step further. We cannot remain content with the interplay of foreground and background, black square and white ground. The further step consists in recognizing that the world in which we are located as observers of the work of art is the background against which the work of art, with its internal interplay of foreground and background, stands out. The interplay of foreground and background that is embodied in Malevich's work itself stands out in the form of a work of art against the background of the world in which we find ourselves whenever we view the work.

We naturally tend to overlook our own position when we engage with a work of art. This is why art always has to find a way to make us aware of our own stance towards it, as our attitudes and interpretations of a work of art form an element of its very essence. It is there in order to be understood, to be seen, heard, tasted, etc. What Malevich underlines is that his work is abstract not because it doesn't represent anything (after all, it represents a black square), but because it doesn't represent the kind of object we think of as paradigmatic: the objects of our everyday interaction with things. This everyday world moves completely into the background of our art appreciation and thereby fades away, becomes unknown and unobserved. Malevich sees the emptying of the world as an important effect of his art, an effect with which one is concerned only once one realizes that the seemingly non-objective work is actually a work about objectivity that stands between us and the world.

> Everything happens because the world is unknown to the human being. If the human being were to comprehend the world, then none of this would exist, and the human being would not need first to form a representation of the world. We are always striving to determine the unknown and to form everything that appears into a conceivable "something," while in fact true meaning lies in exactly the opposite: every "nothing" has risen above every "something." What was a nothing becomes "everything," and every "something" has transformed itself into "nothing" and remains "nothing."[93]

Everything appears against a background that does not itself appear. When we become aware of this by comprehending the movement of thought that is motivated by Malevich's work, we understand that the world does not exist. The ultimate background against which everything appears does not itself exist. The *Black Square* symbolically shows us that every object appears in a field of sense while the background of this occurrence does not appear at all. For this reason, the world as it is usually conceived is no longer found in Malevich's suprematism. It is only in this way that he achieves the desired effect of emptying the world. He frees us from the obsessive idea that there is an all-encompassing field of sense in which everything must be integrated. He overcomes the compulsion to integrate, which consists in the assumption that there is conceptual order that must place all existing things together.

Diversity

This pressure to encompass everything in thought is nicely criticized in *Salami Aleikum* or in Schlingensief's *The German Chainsaw Massacre*. Both of these movies are successful critiques of the idea of integration by showing us that there is no such thing as a unitary German society into which everybody must be assimilated. Our society is not a single block in which all are already equal and from which are excluded a few strangers or foreigners who might be accommodated if they know how to integrate themselves. Not only are there significant cultural differences between East and West Germany, but every state and every city has its own character. In addition, German society is subdivided into subcultures, age groups, and social groups. Society is always a really colorful diversity of perspectives and not a given unity in which alleged foreigners must be incorporated. The idea of a foreigner is already a confusion between a set of legal statuses and something more fundamental, such as the idea that "foreigners" come from "different cultures" and, therefore, do not really belong "here" – as if Germany (or any other country) was more than a legal entity, as if, on top of the legal norms that define a country, there was also a profound ideological unity or harmony in opinions and behavior expected by those who want to reside there. We should finally overcome the idea of national cultures, the fantasy that there is a well-defined entity such as German, British, or American culture. If anything, there are moral values in which the law of a given country is grounded, but conceiving these as local traditions would undermine their supposed objectivity.

The recognition of the fact that others think and live differently regardless of their subsumption under national categories is the first step towards overcoming a compulsive thought that would like to embrace everything. To put it bluntly: if someone behaves in an immoral or just in a rude way and happens to look different from the majority of people in a certain place, it does not follow that the person behaved in an immoral or rude way because he or she looks different. To put it even more bluntly: there are assholes of all colors, races (if this term can even be applied to human beings . . .), religions, genders, nations, etc. This is why democracy is opposed to totalitarianism, because it consists in the recognition that there is no final, all-encompassing truth that tells us exactly how to live, but only a management of perspectives organized by the rule of law. The basic democratic idea of the equality of human beings claims, among other things, that we are equal insofar as we all see things in different ways. This is why we have a right to freedom of opinion. Of course, this does not mean that all perspectives are actually equally true or equally good. That is why we discuss things with each other and practice science or art, in order to find out which views are good and which should be rejected.

The artistic destruction of the fantasy that there is an all-encompassing order consists in the recognition of objects in their interconnections, without thereby isolating them and taking them to be things that simply exist independently of contrast. Nothing merely exists, but everything is found in fields of sense. The black square appears in a field of sense that appears in the painting.

The painting itself frames its objects. This frame indicates that it deals with objects in a particular field of sense.

Against this background it is also noteworthy that in his painting Vermeer frames the scene of the girl reading the letter in many different ways. The painting is thoroughly overcrowded with different frames and framings: the open window through which light infiltrates, the window frame, which in turn consists of many small panes that are individually framed, the frame of the painting, the opened curtains, etc. Even the letter itself is, to a certain extent, a frame in which a text appears, and the fruit bowl is a frame in which fruits appear.

In modernity, the discovery of the never-ending diversity of perspectives is an achievement of the Baroque, and it is central to the work of Georg Wilhelm Leibniz. In one of his main philosophical works, the *Monadology*, he claims that there are an infinite number of perspectives, which, however, harmonize with each other. In a much quoted passage Leibniz writes:

> Just as the same city viewed from different directions appears entirely different and, as it were, multiplied perspectively, in just the same way it happens that, because of the infinite multitude of simple substances, there are, as it were, just as many different universes, which are, nevertheless, only perspectives on a single one, corresponding to the different points of view of each monad.[94]

Here one must always keep in mind that perspectives are not just opinions or subjective ways of looking at an aperspectival objective reality. The visual perspective is itself an objective structure, whose mathematical laws are explored in Renaissance painting and, in the Baroque, lead to the discovery of modern methods that are able to deal with the mathematically infinite. Leibniz actually discovered the calculus at the same time as Isaac

Newton. In the Baroque the world becomes infinite; it diversifies itself into manifold frames. This pluralism of perspectives is also explored in Vermeer's paintings.

On the one hand, with the great scientific revolutions of the last five hundred years modernity promoted the impression of the "readability of the world," which Hans Blumenberg has worked out in comprehensive studies.[95] On the other hand, it became clear already in early modernity that, with scientific progress, the perspectives on the world multiplied, so that it could no longer readily be decided which perspectives should be given priority. This led to the discovery of the infinite in many fields, and it could even be said that we are still working on coming to terms with the infinite in an adequate way. What is crucial here is that the infinite is not just the object of our thinking, but that it also reveals itself in the fact that there are an infinite number of perspectives on the infinite.

Here it must once again be emphasized that this does not make all perspectives equally true or equally good. I am certainly not committing to this or to any other form of relativism that would undermine the objectivity of our knowledge. We make errors by sometimes placing objects in improper fields of sense. Error is also a field of sense, which does not mean that it does not exist. This is why the idea behind perspectivism is misleading, even though it points in the right direction. PERSPECTIVISM is the thesis that there are various perspectives on reality. It is typically assumed that there is a single objective reality to which all perspectives refer. There are different varieties of perspectivism. On the one hand there is objective perspectivism and, on the other, subjective perspectivism. *Objective perspectivism* assumes that the perspectives themselves are objective and are not distortions of reality. In contrast, *subjective perspectivism* views perspectives as a kind of fiction which we create, say, for the sake of survival. It interprets perspectives as "lies in a nonmoral sense," to quote Nietzsche – who was arguably considering subjective perspectivism at the time.[96]

Both options are wrong for many reasons. Objective perspectivism *overestimates* the capacity for truth of the perspectives by defining them in such a way that, in the end, they ultimately refer to a non-perspectival reality. Subjective perspectivism, on the other hand, *underestimates* the capacity for truth of perspectives by taking them to constitute a kind of veil that prevents us from getting hold of reality. Both positions understand perspectives in a one-sided way from the human point of view. In opposition to this tendency, the ontology of fields of sense which I propose understands human perspectives as adding to the stock of ontological facts.

Because the world does not exist, an infinite number of fields of sense exist into which we are thrown and between which we invent and discover connections. We produce new fields of sense as extensions of given ones. Yet this production is in no way a creation from nothing but, rather, is only another alteration in the given structure of fields of sense. We live together in infinitely many fields of sense which we are always rendering intelligible in new ways. What more could we want?

VII

Closing Credits: Television

It seems to be a part of our biological inheritance that we rely heavily on our sense of vision. The traditional canon of the five senses – systematized by Aristotle in his treatise *On the Soul* – famously lists sight, hearing, smell, taste, and touch. As a matter of fact, Aristotle held the peculiar view that touch is somehow fundamental. Yet, ever since Plato, vision is typically treated as our most distinguished sense. And, indeed, as a sense of distance, it places us in a position to determine most accurately which properties of a potentially life-threatening object are most relevant for our survival without having to let the object or predator approach too closely. As such it is a particular distinction and an expression of esteem that we have given a human invention and activity the name of "television."* Television has become a fundamental mode of appropriating reality, of creating and receiving images of what there is. Because of television and its improvement in the aftermath of the digital revolution, we are more than ever constantly surrounded by images and can view events remote from us in both time and space – which is the literal meaning of "television."

Television newscasts report on wars and horrific

---

* In German, television is literally "to see" (sehen) from "afar" (fern). It is seeing at a distance, "Fernsehen."

scenarios of all kinds but also provide us with images of almost superhuman athletic achievements as well as weather forecasts, thereby celebrating our distance from and symbolic control over these events. Luckily war usually takes place somewhere else, at least for those in the position to enjoy the leisure to view it on television. Even though we all know that the "virtual reality" of television often creates appearances that can be deceptive, which are regularly manufactured in order to manipulate us into certain beliefs, it is important to bear in mind that TV has created a massively effective distance machine that outperforms museums, theatres, and cinemas. One often turns on the radio only if one is not able to watch television, such as in the car or if one wants to resist TV for some reason or other. But all of this just testifies to its incredible power.

It should be no surprise that recent TV series have become the main ideological medium. The classical motion picture cannot match what the so-called quality series can achieve: they turn us into junkies, they make us dependent upon them, they function like drugs. Many series reflect and even consciously re-enact this relationship by constructing their plot around the intricacies of drug trafficking. Just think of *The Sopranos*, *The Wire*, *Breaking Bad*, or *Boardwalk Empire*. *The Sopranos* turns you into an addict, in the same way that their protagonists are addicted to women, heroin, or simply pasta, sausage, and wine. A television series can last over eighty hours, which allows much more room to develop a character in the narrative, on account of which *The Sopranos* has been compared with such influential novels as Proust's *In Search of Lost Time*.[97]

Intelligent and successful series such as *Seinfeld*, *The Sopranos*, *Doctor Who*, *Breaking Bad*, *Mad Men*, *Curb Your Enthusiasm*, *The Wire*, *The Office*, or *Louie* – just to name some of my personal favorites – contain deep and far-reaching diagnoses of the spirit of the time. They function as a mirror of our era, a fact in turn reflected in some series, such as the British *Black Mirror*, which is *indeed* an abysmal mirror of the current reality of our media democracies. Ironically, in the first episode, the UK prime minister is forced to have sex live on national television with a pig.

Of course the medium of film has not yet been completely overtaken. It has once more reconceived its own possibilities in recent movies such as *The Artist* or, in David Cronenberg's *Cosmopolis*, taken up a large-scale diagnosis of the current state of capitalism. However, it is American television series in particular that set the tone when it comes to defining an ideological image of our time. They reflect and in large part define how we conceive of ourselves and the alleged overall social order. They shape our sense of what is funny, our *sense of humor*, and thereby have access to our unconscious and its relation to our desire.

One of the good effects of this in Germany is that laughing is no longer frowned upon, even if, with just a few series of really respectable quality, such as *Stromberg* (the German *The Office*) or the profoundly brilliant *KDD – Kriminaldauerdienst*, German TV is a long way from being an ideological market leader. There is no question that the American "culture industry" sets the tone. This is an important element in any explanation of the soft power of the USA in a global economy, as its culture has shaped our viewing habits since at least the end of the Second World War in a massive and effective way. The dominance of the media secures the status of the victor following the Cold War much more than a factual leading position in economic matters: control of the world picture is always a central factor of power in the globalized world.[98]

A *Show about Nothing*

Contemporary TV series raise an age-old question in a new form: is our life more accurately described as a comedy or a tragedy? Do the existential analyses of our favorite television shows correspond with philosophical considerations that are familiar to us?

Heidegger and other existentialists such as Kierkegaard describe our existence more as a tragedy than a comedy. In his famous book *Being and Time*, Heidegger even tried to convince us that we are fundamentally "being-towards-death." We achieve what he thought of as authenticity under the condition that we experience every moment in light of our impending death. "Live as though you were already dead" is in my eyes, however, not an especially recommendable life maxim (which one can also learn from *Breaking Bad*, whose protagonist is doomed to death and loses himself in a mire of drugs). In a similar tone, Kierkegaard claimed that we are stuck in "despair," "sin," and "anxiety." This corresponds to Lars von Trier's diagnosis in his movie *Melancholia*, which portrays the last moments before the extinction of humanity due to another planet's imminent collision with earth. Here, one has to take into account how von Trier cleverly identifies this perspective with sadism. For it is no coincidence that the depressive protagonist of *Melancholia* (played by Kirsten Dunst) is called Justine, which is an allusion to a book by the Marquis de Sade.[99]

Despite the constant threat we have already encountered under the heading of modern nihilism, there is no reason to be infected by existential depression. In *The Sopranos*, existentialism in this sense strikes only Anthony Junior, who makes Nietzsche and Sartre responsible for his clumsy effort to kill himself, but who in truth has a completely different motive than his adolescent existentialism. Existential misery arises when one expects something from life that just doesn't exist, namely immortality, eternal happiness, and an answer to all of our questions. If one approaches life in this way, then one will definitely be disappointed. The same could be said if one expected one's life to be significant and meaningful only if the universe would underscore our efforts at making sense of our existence. But this is just an illusion.

Against exaggerated and misguided expectations on such a grand metaphysical scale (and the unavoidable whining associated with this), *Seinfeld* has taught us that a "show about nothing" need not be meaningless or tragic. The popular sitcom ran from 1989 to 1998 in nine seasons. Without going into the details of the series, suffice it to recall the show's stage setting. A group of friends in New York centered around the comedian Jerry Seinfeld constantly discuss their absurd experiences in relation to the contingencies of their social life. All characters in the series have relationship and commitment issues. In the end this is the only thing that holds Jerry, Kramer, George, and Elaine together. In the fourth season, George Costanza comes up with the idea of pitching a show to NBC, after they approached Jerry, in which they would simply represent their everyday life. In other words, within the show, the protagonists plan to direct a "show." Towards this end George promotes his idea to the potential producers as a *show about nothing*, using that precise statement. The series is about nothing. *Seinfeld* shows that the show is about nothing but itself. It is not about anything else. There is no deeper hidden meaning, and there is no need for any deeper meaning in order to have a great show. Its meaning is entirely superficial. As such the series turns against metaphysics, which assumes that behind the world in which we live a true reality must be hidden, whether this be the reality of physics or some other mystical truth. However, in order for events to have a meaning in the show, it need not go beyond itself and display a hidden purpose. The show needs only itself as its own content. It does not refer to anything beyond itself but, rather, consistently turns towards itself (just as its narcissistic characters do). *Seinfeld* is a series just about itself with the extra paradoxical feature of displaying this reflexive fact within the show.

One of the producers of *Seinfeld*, Larry David, went on to create his own sitcom, *Curb Your Enthusiasm*. It goes a decisive step further than *Seinfeld* in that it is not only about nothing but also about how Larry, one of the original producers of the show about nothing (*Seinfeld*), attempts to give his everyday life some meaning. At one point he attempts to win back his wife, who has left him, by directing a new season of *Seinfeld* and by having her play the wife of George Costanza on an imaginary *Seinfeld* reunion. Within a show about the producer of a show about nothing, a reunion of the show about nothing is staged without ever taking place outside of this staging in its own meta-show.

The characters of *Curb Your Enthusiasm* are no longer simply thrown into a show about nothing, about which they (and we as viewers) can laugh. Instead it becomes clear that they are now producing the show themselves. Larry David adds an additional point to the self-referential aspect of *Seinfeld*, namely that we are responsible for our own destiny, while the characters of *Seinfeld* are more like heroes in a Greek tragedy, as they are victims, as it were, of the contingencies of their own personalities. Indeed, they are comic and can laugh about themselves and everyone else, but they are not successful in developing a moral stance that accounts for their own self-referential activity. *Curb Your Enthusiasm* goes beyond this by introducing a serious dimension that shows society as the domain in which centers of self-reference meet and come to terms with one another.

It is not sufficient to laugh about self-reference.

Were we to laugh only about the fact that we are spiritual beings who are constantly managing our lives on account of the abyss of our radical freedom, we would probably arrive at best at *exasperated laughter*.

In a way, what I suggest is that we move from *Sein* (which in German means "being") to *Seinfeld* (which in German means "field of being"), and from there to *Curb Your Enthusiasm*. We have to learn to take contexts into account rather than believe that all objects, persons, and events are already parts of a grand whole (be it the world itself or even a smaller whole such as society). The question is in what way we can see our life – our collective social life – as a comedy without in the process having to forfeit meaning.

The Senses . . .

Not all laughter overcomes nihilism, as the series *Louie*, in critical contrast to *Curb Your Enthusiasm*, makes apparent. As with *Seinfeld*, *Louie* is about the everyday life of a New York comedian, in this case Louis C. K. The series unfolds in an analogous manner to *Curb Your Enthusiasm*, whose authority, however, it undermines. Larry David constantly puts his foot in his mouth by alluding to social conventions and attempting to change them – sometimes even successfully. In contrast, Louie fails and time and time again lands in the worst situations. He is assaulted more than once, fails helplessly in all matters of romance, and experiences an everyday horror: he meets a child who eats only raw meat and shits in his bathtub. On another occasion Louie becomes the cause of the beheading of a homeless person on the street in New York. Frightened by the homeless person approaching him, Louie pushes him away, whereupon he falls down and is run over by a truck. To the horror of the spectators, his head rolls across the street, which is really an extreme moment in a comedy show. This is the principle of Louis C. K.'s humor: to go a step too far and thereby show, so to speak, the ugly grimace of Larry David.

Of course, one could write an entire library concerning the depiction of the spirit of the times in television series. It would be an intellectual crime just to criticize them as cultural-industrial forms of mass entertainment. Sometimes things are made too easy if a series is reduced to its manipulative characters and the stale difference between high and low culture is reproduced.

In conclusion, I would like to raise one last question, which is connected to the success of television series and the function of television. How are fields of sense actually related to our senses, and how does understanding this relation shed some light on the question concerning the meaning or meaninglessness of our life?

We are accustomed to believing that we have five senses and, on top of that, reason, or the capacity for thinking, that we employ in order to collect, order, and interpret the data relayed to us by our senses. We know that other animals also have other senses and that many of them share some of our senses, but with higher informational resolution (just think of vision in birds). So far, so good. Still, who told us that we have only five senses? Why limit our senses to five, and why not treat thinking or reason as just another sense? What is a "sense" anyway?

As I have already mentioned, the classification of our sense goes back to ancient Greek philosophy, especially to Aristotle's treatise *On the Soul*. Aristotle (as Plato before him) opposes thinking to sensing: thinking coordinates our various senses and refers them to one single object. When I see, touch, smell, or taste an ice cream, thinking and not my senses tells me that the various senses are presenting me with the same object. This is Plato's and Aristotle's reason for distinguishing thinking from sensing. But why not say that thinking itself is a sense, a sense coordinating the other senses in a form of constant synthesis? Why are the senses (or even our body as a whole) opposed to thinking?

It is remarkable that we accept only very few of Aristotle's knowledge claims in the realm of natural science (no one should believe the details of his account of animals in his zoological writings), yet we have so internalized the fundamentals of *On the Soul* that we still interpret our connection to external natural reality as Aristotle did. But there would have been alternatives. Some ancient Indian philosophers already interpreted thought as one of the senses. And in everyday life we sometimes express ourselves by saying that someone has a sense of humor or a sense of height and thereby add senses to the traditional five.

In this connection one can understand a sense as a way in to reality that has the capacity of getting things right or wrong. This is, then, why sight and smell are senses: they provide us with information, and they can in and of themselves guide us in the right direction or mislead us. They do not turn into information sources only because we interpret what they are telling us. Our access to any field of sense, to any reality, is through our senses, including our thinking. It smells like dog food, but it is just a very poorly prepared coq au vin; it feels like silk, but it is an imitation; it seems true to us that some world leader should win a Nobel prize, but we misjudge, etc.

How does this expanded understanding of our senses relate to the discussion of new realism in this book? The answer is just as obvious as it may be surprising. It is just that our senses are not at all subjective. They are not stuck under or on our skin but are objective structures in which we find ourselves. When we hear someone knocking on the door, we comprehend an objective structure and not a sense impression located within our body. For one does not knock in our body, but on the door. We are locked up neither in our skulls nor in our souls. The usual physiology of the senses or the ancient theory of the soul, which unfortunately continues to guide even some of the best neuroscientists to the present day, treats us as though we all suffered from locked-in syndrome, as the protagonist in Julian Schnabel's film *The Diving-Bell and the Butterfly* or the protagonist in the classic anti-war film *Johnny Got His Gun*. Our senses "just ain't in the head," as Hilary Putnam once wrote about the meaning of linguistic utterances.[100]

Once again: when I see passengers boarding a train, I see the passengers and not my mental representations of them. Thus, my sense of vision must belong to reality. It cannot stand outside of that which it sees. This also applies to our sense of orientation. Our senses provide us with pathways through the infinite.

And our thinking expands much further than our sense of vision, for it can engage with the infinite itself. In television, through the sense of sight we are led beyond vision, without thereby necessarily noticing that it also allows television to perform the kind of manipulative function that has been scrutinized by its postmodern critics.

Everything that we know we know through a sense, which has to include the sense of thinking. But this does not mean that our senses are within our body. Senses are "out there," "in reality," or "in actuality," just like mice and fruit trees. In particular, this means that we must reassess the function of our sense of distance, our sense of vision. For it is the sense of sight conceived of in the traditional way that misleads us into believing that we are located in a giant space-time container whose dimensions we can determine via lighting conditions or other radiation of invisible wavelength. It is not by chance that the speed of light has become the metaphysical unit employed to figure out the extent and expansion of the universe conceived of as an immense container. Yet note that Einstein made many discoveries on the basis of pure thought experiments, thereby indeed using thinking as a sense, as successful thought experiments do not consist of mere mental representations. Thought experiments really work. When we discover complex facts through a thought experiment, we engage our sense of thought which, just like all other senses, is both capable of truth and prone to error.

We are always making our way through the infinite. Everything we know is an aspect of the infinite, which is itself neither a whole nor a super-object. We are participating in a sense explosion, because our senses extend to the furthest corners of the universe. As soon as we come to appreciate this, we are able to reject the thought that we are ants in the middle of nowhere. Indeed, we must all die (at least, this is still the case at the time I am writing these lines). And no one can doubt that there is much evil and absurd unnecessary suffering. Still, we may also come to see that everything can be otherwise than the way it appears to us, simply because everything that exists appears simultaneously in infinitely many fields of sense. Nothing is simply the way that we perceive it to be but, rather, is infinitely more – a comforting thought.

Television can free us from the illusion that there is one single all-encompassing world. In a television series or a film we can develop different perspectives on a situation. In contrast to theatre, we are not sitting in front of a stage. Movies are lenses into the past too, for there we can see deceased actors continuing to exist as spectres on the screen. In a radical sense, film is a "show about nothing," an engagement with the diversity of interpretive possibilities beyond the fixed idea that there is a single world in which everything happens and which determines what is real and what is fiction. To recognize this plurality of perspectives, without positing an unnecessary unification, is exactly the point of modern freedom (and modern television).

After all, it is joyful news that the world does not exist. For it allows us to conclude our reflections with an emancipatory smile. There is no super-object to which we must surrender in our lifetime. Instead, we are enmeshed in infinite possibilities which draw the infinite close to us. For only in this way is it possible that everything exists which in fact exists.

... and the Meaning of Life

My answer to the question "What is the meaning of being?," to take up a famous formulation of Heidegger, is the ontology of fields. The meaning of being, the meaning of the expression "being," or rather "existence," is sense itself. This is revealed in the non-existence of the world. The non-existence of the world triggers an explosion of sense. For everything exists only because it appears in a field of sense. Because an all-encompassing field of sense cannot exist, there exist an unlimited plurality of fields of sense. It is not the case that all fields of sense are somehow connected with each other, because otherwise the world would exist in the form of an infinitely related network. The connections between fields of sense, which we observe and bring about ourselves, are made up of new fields of sense. We cannot escape sense. Sense is our destiny, as it were.

The answer to the question concerning the meaning of life lies in sense itself. That there are infinitely many senses, which we can know and change, is already the meaning we are looking for. Or, to put it in a nutshell: the meaning of life is the engagement with infinite sense, in which we are fortunately able to participate. That we are not always happy with the process is self-evident. That unhappiness and unnecessary suffering exist is also true and should present us with an opportunity to think ourselves anew and to improve ourselves morally. Against this background it is certainly important to bring clarity to our ontological situation, because humanity is always changing in light of its conception of the fundamental structure of reality. The next step consists in giving up the search for an all-encompassing structure. Instead we should build communities that help us better understand the many existing structures in a way that is more creative and free of bias, so that we can more effectively judge what should remain as it is and what should be changed. Just because everything exists does not mean that all is well or that all existing things or structures are somehow equally valid. We find ourselves together on a great expedition – we have arrived here from nowhere, and together we set out into the infinite.

Notes

1 For these "historical" details, see also Maurizio Ferraris, *Introduction to the New Realism*, trans. Sarah de Sanctis. London: Bloomsbury, 2015.

2 Heinrich von Kleist, letter of 22 March 1801 to Wilhelmine von Zenge, in *The Broken Jug*, trans. Roger Jones. Manchester: Manchester University Press, 1977, p. vi.

3 Slavoj Žižek, *Less than Nothing: Hegel and the Shadow of Dialectical Materialism*. London: Verso, 2012.

4 Ludwig Wittgenstein, *Tractatus Logico-Philosophicus*, trans. C. K. Ogden. Mineola, NY: Dover, 1999, p. 27.

5 Compare Plato, *The Apology*, in *Five Dialogues*, trans. G. M. A. Grube. Indianapolis: Hackett, 2002, p. 27 (23b).

6 See Viktor Pelevin, *Buddha's Little Finger*, trans. Andrew Bromfield. New York: Penguin, 1999, pp. 140–1.

7 See Brian Greene, *The Elegant Universe: Superstrings, Hidden Dimensions, and the Quest for the Ultimate Theory*. New York: W.W. Norton, 2003.

8 Arthur Schopenhauer, *The World as Will and*

Representation, Vol. 2, trans. E. F. J. Payne. Mineola, NY: Dover, ch. 1, p. 3.

9 Friedrich Nietzsche, *Beyond Good and Evil*, ch. IV: "Apophthegems and Interludes," aphorism 150, trans. Helen Zimmern. Newstead, Queensland: Emered, 2009.

10 Ludwig Wittgenstein, *Tractatus Logico-Philosophicus*, trans. C. K. Ogden. Mineola, NY: Dover, 1999, p. 29.

11 Friedrich Nietzsche, *Will to Power*, § 481 (1883–8), p. 62, https://archive.org/details/TheWillToPower-Nietzsche.

12 Martin Heidegger, "Aletheia (Heraclitus Fragment B 16)," in *Early Greek Thinking*, trans. David Farrell Krell and Frank A. Capuzzi. New York: Harper & Row, 1975, p. 115.

13 Stephen Hawking, *The Grand Design*. New York: Bantam Books, 2010, p. 5.

14 Jürgen Habermas, *Truth and Justification*, ed. and trans. Barbara Fultner. Cambridge, MA: MIT Press, 2003, pp. 89–90. For the expression "pragmatic presupposition of an objective world," see pp. 33 and 35; for "presupposition of a world of objects," see p. 34.

15 Ibid., p. 57.

16 Ibid., p. 91.

17 Ibid., p. 22.

18 Timothy Williamson, "Past the Linguistic Turn," in Brian Leiter (ed.), *The Future for Philosophy*. Oxford: Clarendon Press, 2004, pp. 106–28.

19 For the latest developments in the debate concerning the delicate connection between philosophy and science, I recommend the work of the great American philosopher Hilary Putnam. His most recent book, *Philosophy in an Age of Science*, offers an especially impressive and very comprehensible overview of his thoughts on the topic. See

Hilary Putnam, *Philosophy in an Age of Science: Physics, Mathematics, and Skepticism*. Cambridge, MA: Harvard University Press, 2012.

20 See Terence Horgan and Matjaz Potrč, "Blobjectivism and Indirect Correspondence," *Facta Philosophica* 2 (2000), pp. 249–70.

21 Jacques Derrida, *Of Grammatology*, trans. Gayatri Chakravorty Spivak. Baltimore: Johns Hopkins University Press, 1997, p. 158.

22 Gottlob Frege, "Sense and Reference," *Philosophical Review* 57/3 (1948), pp. 209–30.

23 Ibid., p. 210.

24 Goethe, *Faust*, trans. Walter Arndt, ed. Cyrus Hamlin. New York: 2nd edn, W. W. Norton, 2001, pp. 192–3.

25 Jean Paul, *Biographie eines Bonmotisten*, in *Historisch-Kritische Gesamtausgabe*, part II, vol. 1, Weimar, 1927, p. 448.

26 Rainer Maria Rilke, excerpt from *The Eighth Duino Elegy*, trans. Robert Hunter, http://www.hunterarchive.com/files/Poetry/Elegies/elegy8.html.

27 See Brian Greene, *The Fabric of the Cosmos: Space, Time, and the Texture of Reality*. New York: Vintage Books, 2004.

28 See Hans Blumenberg, *Work on Myth*, trans. Robert M. Wallace. Cambridge, MA: MIT Press, 1990, p. 25. Regarding Thales, see also Blumenberg's elaborate *The Laughter of the Thracian Woman: A Protohistory of Theory*, trans. Spencer Hawkins. London: Bloomsbury Academic Press, 2015.

29 Martin Heidegger, *Being and Time*, trans. John Macquarrie and Edward Robinson. New York: Harper & Row, 1962, § 14. "The Leap" is the translator's rendering.

30 See Thomas Nagel, *The View from Nowhere*. New York: Oxford University Press, 1986.

31 Rainer Maria Rilke, *Die Gedichte*, Frankfurt am

Main: Insel, 1998, p. 456. See http://poemhunter.
com/poem/childhood-2/.

32 Max Scheler, *The Human Place in the Cosmos*.
Evanston, IL: Northwestern University Press, 2008.

33 See Wolfram Hogrebe, *Risky Proximity to Life:
The Scenic Existence of Homo sapiens*, trans.
Adam Knowles. New York: New School for Social
Research, 2010.

34 Immanuel Kant, *Kritik der reinen Vernunft*.
Stuttgart, 1975, p. 90.

35 Theodor Adorno and Max Horkheimer, *Dialectic
of Enlightenment*, trans. Edmund Jephcott, ed.
Gunzelin Schmid Noerr. Stanford, CA: Stanford
University Press, 2007.

36 See Eduardo Viveiros de Castro, *From the Enemy's
Point of View: Humanity and Divinity in an
Amazonian Society*. Chicago: University of Chicago
Press, 1992; and *The Inconstancy of the Indian
Soul: The Encounter of Catholics and Cannibals
in 16th-Century Brazil*. Chicago: Prickly Paradigm
Press, 2011.

37 Wilfrid Sellars, *Empiricism and the Philosophy of
Mind*. Cambridge, MA: Harvard University Press,
1997, p. 83.

38 Mario De Caro and David Macarthur (eds),
Naturalism in Question. Cambridge, MA: Harvard
University Press, 2008.

39 Hilary Putnam, *Philosophy in the Age of Science*:
Physics, Mathematics, and Skepticism. Cambridge,
MA: Harvard University Press, 2012.

40 Bobby Henderson, *The Gospel of the Flying
Spaghetti Monster*. New York: Villard Books,
2006.

41 See Richard Dawkins, *The God Delusion*. Boston:
Houghton Mifflin, 2006.

42 Genesis 1:1.

43 See Saul A. Kripke, *Naming and Necessity*.

Cambridge, MA: Harvard University Press, 1980, pp. 39–56.

44 Willard Van Orman Quine, "Two Dogmas of Empiricism," *Philosophical Review* 60 (1951), pp. 20–43; repr. in Quine, *From a Logical Point of View*. 2nd rev. edn, Cambridge, MA: Harvard University Press, 1961.

45 Putnam, *Philosophy in an Age of Science*, pp. 41f.

46 See Edwin Bissell Holt, Walter Taylor Marvin, William Pepperell Montague, Ralph Barton Perry, Walter Boughton Pitkin and Edward Gleason Spaulding, *The New Realism: Cooperative Studies in Philosophy*. New York: Macmillan, 1912.

47 Theodore Sider, *Writing the Book of the World*. Oxford: Oxford University Press, 2011, p. 18.

48 Regarding the pre-history of the problem, compare my books *Antike und moderne Skepsis zur Einführung* (Hamburg: Junius, 2008) and *Skeptizismus und Idealismus in der Antike* (Frankfurt am Main: Suhrkamp, 2009).

49 Immanuel Kant, *Critique of Pure Reason*, trans. and ed. Paul Guyer and Allen W. Wood. New York: Cambridge University Press, 2000, B59, A42185.

50 Brian Greene, *The Hidden Reality: Parallel Universes and the Deep Laws of the Cosmos*. New York: Vintage Books, 2011.

51 See Nelson Goodman, *Fact, Fiction, and Forecast*. Cambridge, MA: Harvard University Press, 1983. The best overview of his philosophy can be found in his book *Ways of Worldmaking*. Indianapolis: Hackett, 1978.

52 Martin Heidegger, "The Age of the World Picture," in *The Question Concerning Technology and Other Essays*, trans. William Lovitt. New York: Harper & Row, 1977, pp. 129–30.

53 See Paul Boghossian, *Fear of Knowledge: Against*

Relativism and Constructivism. Oxford: Oxford University Press, 2007, and Quentin Meillassoux, *After Finitude: An Essay on the Necessity of Contingency*, trans. Ray Brassier. London: Bloomsbury Academic, 2010.

54 Shakespeare, *Hamlet*, Act I, scene v.

55 See Sigmund Freud, *The Joke and its Relation to the Unconscious*, trans. Joyce Crick. London: Penguin.

56 See Jacques Derrida, *Of Spirit: Heidegger and the Question*. Chicago: University of Chicago Press, 1991.

57 Hans-Georg Gadamer, *Truth and Method*. 2nd edn, trans. Joel Weinsheimer and Donald G. Marshall. New York: Crossroad, 1992.

58 Werner Heisenberg, *Physics and Philosophy: The Revolution in Modern Science*. London: Allen & Unwin, 1958, pp. 97–8.

59 Max Weber, "Science as a Vocation," *Daedalus* 87/1 (1958), pp. 111–34.

60 Ibid., p. 117.

61 Ibid., p. 133.

62 Friedrich Schleiermacher, *On Religion: Speeches to its Cultured Despisers*, trans. and ed. Richard Crouter. Cambridge: Cambridge University Press, 1997, p. 23.

63 Ibid., p. 19.

64 Ibid., p. 100.

65 Ibid., p. 27.

66 Ibid., p. 52.

67 Ibid., p. 54.

68 Ibid., pp. 103–4.

69 Friedrich Nietzsche, *Thus Spake Zarathustra*, trans. Thomas Common, Project Gutenberg, 7 November 2008, http://www.gutenberg.org/files/1998/1998-h/1998-h.htm#link2H_4_0008. From section III, *Backworldsmen*. Here Nietzsche

cleverly plays on the terms "Hinterweltler" and "Hinterwäldler," which are more or less homophone. The latter is a term for people living "at the back of beyond," "behind the woods," while a "Hinterwelt" is a "shadow world." The conflation "Hinterweltler" is Nietzsche's invention.

70 Karl Marx, *Capital*, Vol. 1, trans. S. Moore and E. Aveling, in *The Marx–Engels Reader*, ed. R. C. Tucker. 2nd edn, New York: W. W. Norton, 1978, pp. 320–1.

71 Romans 11:13.

72 Martin Heidegger, *Contributions to Philosophy (of the Event)*, trans. Richard Rojcewicz and Daniela Vallega-Neu. Bloomington: Indiana University Press, 2012, p. 315.

73 Alva Noë, *Out of our Heads: Why You are Not your Brain, and Other Lessons from the Biology of Consciousness*. New York: Hill & Wang, 2009.

74 Søren Kierkegaard, *The Sickness Unto Death*. London: Penguin, 2008, p. 45: "for God is the fact that everything is possible, or that everything is possible is God."

75 In a famous letter to Ferdinand Tönnies dated 2 March 1909, Max Weber writes: "It is true that I am absolutely unmusical in matters religious and that I have neither the need nor the ability to erect any religious edifices within me – that is simply impossible for me, and I reject it. But after examining myself carefully I must say that I am neither antireligious nor irreligious." See Guenther Roth and Wolfgang Schluchter, *Max Weber's Version of History: Ethics and Models*. Berkeley: University of California Press, 1979, p. 82n.

76 For example, Gottlob Frege, "Logik in der Mathematik," in *Nachgelassene Schriften*, ed. H. Hermes, F. Kambartel and F. Kaulbach. Hamburg: Meiner, 1983, pp. 243, 250.

77 Stanley Cavell, *The World Viewed: Reflections on the Ontology of Film*. Enlarged edn, Cambridge, MA: Harvard University Press, 1979, p. 85.

78 Gottlob Frege, "Sense and Reference," *Philosophical Review* 57/3 (1948), p. 210.

79 Ibid., p. 213.

80 See Stéphane Mallarmé, "The Demon of Analogy," in *Collected Poems*, trans. Henry Weinfield. Berkeley: University of California Press, 1994, pp. 93–5. I thank Wolfram Hogrebe for referring me to this piece.

81 Ibid., p. 93.

82 Ibid.

83 Ibid., p. 94.

84 Ibid.

85 Ibid.

86 For a similar interpretation, see Wolfram Hogrebe, "Metafisica Povera," in Tilman Borsche and Werner Stegmaier (eds), *Zur Philosophie des Zeichens*. Berlin and New York, 1992, pp. 79–101.

87 Wilfrid Sellars, *Empiricism and the Philosophy of Mind*. Cambridge, MA: Harvard University Press, 1997, p. 40.

88 Mallarmé, "The Demon of Analogy," p. 94.

89 Sigmund Freud, *The Joke and its Relation to the Unconscious*, trans. A. A. Brill. London: Kegan Paul, Trench, Trubner.

90 J. M. Masson (ed.), *The Complete Letters of Sigmund Freud to Wilhelm Fliess, 1887–1904*. Cambridge, MA: Harvard University Press, 1985, p. 290.

91 Freud, *The Joke and its Relation to the Unconscious*, pp. 269–70.

92 Ibid., p. 193.

93 See Kazimir Malewitsch, *The Non-objective World*, trans. Howard Dearstyne. Chicago: Paul Theobald, 1959.

94 Leibniz, *The Monadology*, ed. and trans. Daniel Garber and Roger Ariew. Indianapolis: Hackett, 1991, p. 76.
95 See Hans Blumenberg, *The Legitimacy of the Modern Age*. Cambridge, MA: MIT Press, 1985; also, in particular, his *Die Lesbarkeit der Welt*. Frankfurt am Main: Suhrkamp, 1986.
96 Friedrich Nietzsche, "On Truth and Lies in a Nonmoral Sense," in *The Nietzsche Reader*, ed. Keith Ansell-Pearson and Duncan Large. Oxford: Blackwell, 2006, pp. 114–24.
97 See Diedrich Diederichsen, *The Sopranos*, Zurich: Diaphenes, 2012.
98 See, for example, ibid., p. 52.
99 Donatien Alphonse François de Sade, *Justine, or, The Misfortunes of Virtue*. Oxford: Oxford University Press, 2012.
100 Hilary Putnam, "The Meaning of 'Meaning,'" *Minnesota Studies in the Philosophy of Science* 7 (1975), pp. 131–93.

Glossary

ABSOLUTE DIFFERENCE: A difference between an object and all other objects.

ABSOLUTE IDEALISM: The thesis that a super-thought exists.

APPEARANCE: "Appearance" designates a general expression for "to be found in" or "occurrence." Appearances can be abstract entities, such as numbers, or concrete, material entities, such as material things.

BLOBJECTIVISM: The double thesis that there is only a single all-encompassing domain of objects and that this domain of objects is itself an object.

CONSTRUCTIVISM: The fundamental assumption that no facts or things exist in themselves at all, and that we construct all facts through multifarious discourses or scientific methods.

CREATIONISM: The thesis that God's intervention in nature explains nature better than the natural sciences.

DIAGONAL PREDICATE: A predicate that runs diagonally across the Sider world, namely a predicate that organizes the world in absurd ways.

DUALISM: The conception that exactly two substances exist – that is, two kinds of objects. In particular, it entails the assumption that thinking and matter are completely differentiated from one another.

ERROR THEORY: A theory that explains the systematic error in a domain of discourse and traces this back to a series of erroneous assumptions.

EXISTENCE: The property of fields of sense, namely that something exists in them.

EXISTENTIALISM: The investigation into human existence.

FACT: Something that is true about something.

FACTICITY: The fact that there is something rather than nothing – that is, that there exists anything at all.

FETISHISM: The projection of supernatural powers onto an object that one has created oneself.

FIELDS OF SENSE: The places in which everything appears.

FIRST MAIN PRINCIPLE OF POSITIVE ONTOLOGY: There exist an infinite number of fields of sense.

FRACTAL ONTOLOGY: The claim that the non-existence of the world arises once again in the form of small copies of the world. Every other isolated object is like the world. Because the world does not exist, the great problem of the world repeats itself on a small scale.

GOD: The idea that the whole is meaningful, although it transcends our apprehension.

HERMENEUTICAL CONSTRUCTIVISM: A constructivism which asserts that all interpretations of texts are constructions. According to this view, texts have meaning only relative to interpretation and not in and of themselves.

MAIN PRINCIPLE OF NEGATIVE ONTOLOGY: The world does not exist.

MATERIALISM: The claim that everything that exists is material.

MATERIALISTIC MONISM: A position which holds that the universe is the only existing domain of objects and that identifies this with the totality of material objects that can be explained by appealing to laws of nature alone.

MENTAL REPRESENTATIONALISM: The assumption that we do not perceive things directly but only ever grasp them as spiritual mental images without ever being able to have direct access to them.

MEREOLOGICAL SUM: The construction of a whole through the unification of several parts.

MEREOLOGY: A domain of logic that concerns itself with the formal relations between wholes and their parts.

METAPHYSICS: The attempt to develop a theory of the whole world.

MODERN NIHILISM: The claim that in the end everything is meaningless.

MONAD: A maximally self-sufficient object that is completely independent of all other objects by having a determinate and limited number of properties.

MONISM: The assumption of a single substance, of a super-object that contains all other objects within itself.

NATURALISM: The claim that only nature exists and

that it is identical with the universe, the subject matter of the natural sciences.

NEW REALISM: The double thesis that, first, we can know things in themselves and, second, that things and facts in themselves do not belong to a single domain of objects.

NOMINALISM: The thesis that our concepts and categories do not copy or describe structures or divisions of the world, but that all concepts which we human beings make of ourselves or our environment are only generalizations that we carry out in order to increase our chances of survival.

OBJECT: What we think about with truth-apt thoughts. Not all objects are spatio-temporal things; numbers and dreamscapes are also objects in a formal sense.

OBJECT DOMAIN: A domain, containing a particular kind of object, in which there obtain rules that connect these objects with one another.

ONTOLOGICAL PROVINCE: A region of the whole which should not be confused with the whole itself.

ONTOLOGICAL REDUCTION: An ontological reduction is undertaken when one discovers that an allegedly objective domain of discourse is – basically – mere idle talk.

ONTOLOGY: Traditionally, the expression signifies the doctrine of beings. In this book, "ontology" is understood as the analysis of the meaning of existence.

ONTOLOGY OF FIELDS OF SENSE: This claims that, whenever a field of sense can be found in which it appears, there is something rather than nothing.

PERSPECTIVISM: The thesis that there exist various perspectives on reality.

PHYSICALISM: The assumption that all existing things are found in the universe and for this reason can be investigated by physics.

PLURALISM: Many substances exist (and, in any case, significantly more than two).

PRINCIPLE OF HOMO MENSURA: The human being is the measure of all things.

REALISM: The thesis that, whenever we know anything at all, we know things in themselves.

REFLECTION: Thinking about thinking.

REGISTRY: A selection of premises, media, methods, and materials employed for the sake of acquiring knowledge and processing information.

RELATIVE DIFFERENCE: A difference between one object and several other objects.

RELIGION: A return to ourselves from the infinite, the absolutely unavailable and unchangeable, in which it is important that we do not completely lose ourselves.

SCIENTIA MENSURA PRINCIPLE: Whenever the concern is the description of the world, science is the measure of all things.

SCIENTIFIC REALISM: A theory according to which we know things in themselves (as opposed to mere constructions, for example) by means of scientific theories.

SCIENTISM: The belief that the natural sciences understand the fundamental level of reality, the world in itself, while all other viewpoints are to be measured by them.

SECOND MAIN PRINCIPLE OF POSITIVE ONTOLOGY: Every field of sense is an object. We can think about every field of sense, although we cannot fully comprehend all fields of sense.

SENSE: The way in which an object appears.

STRUCTURAL REALISM: The claim that structures exist.

SUBJECTIVE PREDICATE: A predicate that all subjects – let us say, all people – employ. Predicates that, for instance, can be recognized only by dolphins, because they use echolocation, are examples of subjective predicates.

SUBSTANCE: The bearer of properties.

SUPER-OBJECT: An object that has all possible properties.

SUPER-THOUGHT: The thought that thinks about the whole world and about itself at the same time.

UNIVERSE: The domain of objects accessible to the experimental methods of natural science.

WORLD: The field of sense of all fields of sense; the field of sense in which all other fields of sense appear. The author of this book argues that such a world does not exist.

Index of Names